Unforgotten Exmoor

WORDS AND PICTURES FROM A VANISHED ERA

UNFORGOTTEN EXMOOR

WORDS AND PICTURES FROM A VANISHED ERA

VOLUME ONE

Victor Lock
Blanche (née Watts) & John Pile
Ted Lethaby
Roy Kellaway

DAVID RAMSAY

David Ramsay

RARE BOOKS AND BERRY
2010

First published in 2009
Reprinted 2010

Rare Books and Berry
High Street, Porlock,
Minehead, Somerset
TA24 8PU

www.rarebooksandberry.co.uk

2 4 6 8 10 9 7 5 3

© David Ramsay

A CIP catalogue record for this title is
available from the British Library

ISBN 978-0-9557119-8-5

Designed and typeset in Minion at
Alacrity, Sandford, Somerset

Printed and bound by
The MPG Books Group, Bodmin and King's Lynn

CONDITIONS OF SALE

This book is dedicated to
Ivy and Victor
who started it all off

"What you leave behind is not what is
engraved in stone monuments, but what is
woven into the lives of others."

Pericles

Contents

Acknowledgements

WITH SPECIAL THANKS to Nicky, for all her help and support, comment and feedback. Also to Andrew and Pauline Lyle for extending the idea, and for their unswerving encouragement and belief; and to Philip and Lyn Carey for keeping it going, and their infectious positivity; and to the Percivals, the Sydenhams, the Foxes and the Boyds, and all the other fixers, persuaders, encouragers and cajolers without whom some of the interviews would never have happened at all.

But above all I would like to thank all the people themselves who were willing to talk and enthusiastically share their memories and photographs with me – and race along too! I am very lucky. I hope that putting it all on record will help keep alive and make permanent their remembered past. I also hope that it might in some small way act as a prism through which younger generations and visitors to the area can see and better appreciate the present Exmoor – their Exmoor now – in the same way that listening to and working on these stories has made me see familiar places in such a very different light.

I am deeply grateful to you all.

Victor Lock

Born in 1928 in the back-room at Cranscombe, a farm above Rockford, Victor was the fifth and youngest child in a family that had been at the farm for four generations. He spent the war years finishing his education at Brendon School, and then at the age of fourteen started an apprenticeship as a carpenter in Lynton. After the war he married Margaret Graham from Wilsham, the farm to the north of Cranscombe, and in 1952 they left the area and went to live in Bridgwater, where their daughter Susan was born.

As a boy I used to play with my brother Bill, who was four years older than I was, and the two lads at Shilstone, Colin Sanders and David Back, who lived in the cottage there. We'd go bird-nesting up Tippacott Splats and mess about in the fields – you know, playing bows and arrows, glider planes, that sort of thing. We'd also go fishing, but we'd have to keep an eye open in case we were caught. We'd fish for trout with a rod and worm and would go down through Oaklands Wood. They wouldn't see you there. Anything we caught we'd take home for supper and fry.

Other times we'd go cycling or walking – I always liked going for walks. If weather was bad we'd stay indoors and play cards or dominoes.

In the winter time there'd be proper ice runnels in all the field gutters in the front meadow. It would freeze up and we'd go skating there, right along the gutters.* We also liked to start a little snowball at the top of the field when it had been snowing, and roll it down the hill, and it would end up high as a house sort of thing at the bottom. I didn't like school at first but it got better later.

Cranscombe in the 1940s, with the field gutters clearly visible as parallel lines in the front field

Us kids also had a donkey which we rode a lot. He didn't have a name and was always just called Donkey. We enjoyed riding him, but the problem was only two could fit on at any one time. Usually there were three of us. One day Bill and I came off, and it was because Colin Sanders had tried to ride his bike through the back legs of the

---

* Field gutters were used to irrigate the fields and can still be seen in many parts of Exmoor, grassed over now and running in parallel lines along the contours. Besides irrigation, farmers could also feed their fields by adding dung to the water in the gutters, or lime to sweeten the soil, or ash, which was carefully preserved from the wood or peat house-fires. Gutters first appeared on a few Exmoor farms at the end of the eighteenth century and became common during the next. In the 1850s experiments were carried out to try to fractionally raise the temperature of the ground by using water which came from deep underground springs, rather than water from surface streams, and running this along the gutters: underground spring water was always a constant temperature and in winter was warmer than any surface water. This proved very successful, and the slight increase in warmth encouraged a flush of early grass, or allowed grass to continue growing long after it would normally have died down in the early winter. This system could, of course, only be used on farms which had deep underground springs. The use of field gutters has now almost completely died out.

donkey – he was jealous he wasn't on it himself. Anyway, Donkey kicked up, and over the front we both went. Bill's teeth dug into my head and it caused a lot of damage to both of us. We had to have the doctor up, Dr Head up from Rockford. We were in the old back-house* there, and he was putting some stitches into Bill's chin before he got on to putting stitches into my head, and I was leaning over close to look to see what he was doing. Suddenly he swivelled round and said, "Get out the way there or I'll cut your blithering head off!" I moved quick, I can tell you.

The war started when I was twelve. Suddenly there were a lot of changes. My sister Ivy left and went to South Devon with the land-girls. Two years in and my brother Bill left to join the Navy, and Tom joined the Home Guard. We had conscientious objectors moving in with us and living in rooms in the main house, not just for the summer, like the summer visitors, but permanently. Also, suddenly the place got busy; hundreds of Americans came to Exmoor to train and lived in a camp of Nissen huts which was built at Cross Gate. They used to visit the farm; I don't know what they were doing here but they came round regularly. The training happened behind us on the common and they would have target practice with shells filled with sand and water. They could do a lot of damage, those shells, if they landed in your field. The practice caused quite a bit of disturb-ance, with huge tanks and all the shelling.† The shells would knock out a great big hole when they landed, even though they were just sand and water.

At night you'd hear the German planes flying over the farm. You could tell the German planes because they sounded different to ours, a sort of pulsating sound. They'd be on their way to bomb Wales – the docks and the industrial parts on the other side of the Bristol Channel. You'd see searchlights from Wales criss-crossing the sky and we'd hear the sirens going off. I'd lie in bed at night in my room at the back of the house and could hear the bombs landing, a dull sort of thump, thump in the distance, lots of them, and sometimes you'd even feel the vibrations. Then another sound would start up which was the sound of the anti-aircraft guns, the Welsh trying to shoot down the planes. We had to have good blackouts, even though we only had candles and lamps, because we didn't want even a glimmer

---

* The kitchen.
† The deep tank tracks can still be clearly seen leading onto the common, just to the east of Tippacott Farm, where the common meets the road.

*Brother Tom joined the Home Guard,
pictured here at the gate to Countisbury Church.*

of light to get out. We made frames covered with black linen that fitted the windows tightly.

Another strong memory from the war was getting letters from brother Bill who was in the Navy; Mother would read them to herself first, and then tell us what was in them, where he was and so on. We also had some evacuee children come to the

*Brother Bill, bottom right,
in the Navy.*

13

school; they suddenly arrived in our class. I can remember three of them, but not their names. I think one of them stayed down at Oaklands. They were here quite a long time, if I remember rightly – they must have liked it! Oh yes, when the war started it definitely got busy round here!

I was always expected to help out on the farm when I was at school, as well as after I'd started work, particularly hay harvest and corn harvest, and wherever else I was needed. I'd be expected to go and cut turfs on the common with my brother and father, and to fork the vegetable garden with manure from the stables. These were the sorts of things I was expected to do.

With the turf, or peat, you'd go up to the common and search for the right place. Father knew how to find the places to cut. Of course it would have to be near a track for the horse and cart. All the farmers cut their turf; there were stooks of turfs drying all over. We'd go up for a day at a time to cut it in the early spring, to give it long as possible to dry.

There are two sorts of turf: one we called skin-turf and the other pit-turf, which is what you most probably call peat. The skin-turf was

taken off level with the surface with a blade like a shovel. You'd push it through, you'd shove it through with your stomach, leaning on it. You'd cut it about three inches thick, and a foot wide, and when it was about three feet long you'd tip it over and leave it standing there on its side to dry. Then you'd lift them up into stooks, just in twos to start with, lying side by side to dry out. We'd use these ones at the back of the fire.

The second sort we cut was the pit-turf, and this was the best sort for burning. This was more out in the boggy ground, and you'd find it by the cotton flowers, the cotton grass growing there. The pit-turf we'd spine off, going straight down vertically about three foot into the bog, and at the bottom it would be really black. They would be about nine inches wide and about two inches thick, and the length would all depend on the depth of the bog. Of course you'd have a different sort of turfing spade from the one for the skin-turf, and each one you cut you'd place straight on a barrow until you had about ten to a load. Then you'd wheel them away till you were on dry land. You'd spread them around and you'd have to go back to turn them. When they were dry, the bottoms, which were jet black, would be just like a lump of coal, and it would last a long time. It was dirty, dirty fire-stuff, but it did the job.

*"Happy memories of the harvest, 1932" was written
on the back of this photograph from a holidaymaker.
Tom on the load, Bill on the horse and Father standing.*

When all the turfs were dry we'd bring them down on the horse and cart and build them into a giant rick near the back door of the house, ready for winter. The middle of the rick was hollow to let the air through and the dog would always go there automatically because he could see the door to the house from there. He used the turf-rick as his kennel.

As we grew up, my eldest brother, Tom, was working with Dad on the farm and my sisters were helping Mum with the holidaymakers, so my brother Bill and I had to find something else to do for work. Bill went to the electric light works down at Lynmouth* to train as an electrician, before being called up to the Navy, and when I was fourteen I started an apprenticeship as a carpenter. This was for Mr Nancekivell, who ran the woodwork shop and the undertaking business in Park Street in Lynton. I used to take a push-bike to work, leaving Cranscombe at about seven in the morning and cycling down to Lynmouth to the old coal yard, where I'd leave the bike and walk from there on up to Lynton. The starting wage for an apprentice was 7/6 a week, and I'd give mother 5/- and I had the 2/6.

Of course when I first started I didn't have any tools of my own and I just used the workshop tools. Then, after a couple of months, Mr Nancekivell suggested that he deduct some money from the wages, so much a week, and gradually that way I could build up my own collection of tools. The timber used to arrive rough-sawn, and usually the first job of the day was to hand-plane it all smooth, ready for use. We used the wooden bench planes which were in the workshop, but as soon as we went out on site we needed our own tools.

During the apprenticeship, and after, I used to do two types of work, really. The first was general building work, and sometimes this was in the woodwork shop in Lynton and other times it was out on site. My boss was Master of the Staghounds and he had contacts all over the common, so I worked all over. The worst thing about site work was roofing because the scaffolding wasn't like you'd get today, metal scaffolding. It was wooden poles with the joints tied up with rope. You'd have to put it up yourself before you started, and tie up all the joints. Some of those buildings in Lynton, near the edge, you'd look straight down over the cliff and into the sea! It was really scary on rickety wooden scaffolding with a strong wind blowing!

The second type of work I did was the coffins. They were usually made in elm, but people could order oak if they wanted, and the part that took the time was bending each side of the coffin. You'd make some parallel saw cuts, only going about halfway through the wood, and then you'd plane these out so that there was space for the wood to bend into. Then you'd pour boiling water over the sides as you

---

* In 1890 a hydro-electric plant was installed in the fast-flowing East Lyn River, and Lynton became one of the first places in the country – only eight years after parts of London – to have a public electricity supply for both street lights and domestic use. Contemporary writers visiting Lynton marvelled at the incongruity of thatched houses brightly lit by electricity, and the fact that the very streets of Lynmouth were now lit by the new "electric glow-lamps".

*Unloading coal from a ship at Lynmouth near the old coal yard.
When I started as a carpenter I'd leave my bike at the
yard there and walk up to Lynton.*

worked; one person would be bending the wood and the other would be tapping it into the base, which would keep it in the right shape. It would take two of you a day to make a coffin; it had to be made up, cleaned, sanded and polished, and would be about a day's work. Then you'd put on the brass handles and they had to be strong, especially the ones at either end, the rings at either end, because they were the ones they put the tapes through to lower the coffin into the grave. We'd also make up a template of the coffin for the gravedigger, two inches bigger all round, which he'd use to dig the grave and make sure the coffin wouldn't get wedged halfway down the hole. We'd make up the template as soon as we could so that Mr Nancekivell could deliver it to the graveyard, which gave the gravedigger as much time as possible.

I had to go and measure the body of the deceased before each coffin was made. I'd have to go to the person's home, or sometimes to the little Lynton hospital if they'd died in hospital. I'd usually get the message in the morning. Mr Nancekivell would say, "Mr so-and-so has passed away, can you go up to such-and-such a place and take the measurements." So I set off on my bike if it was a distance, but on foot if it was the hospital. If it was a person's home the relatives were expecting me. They'd always give you a drink, a whisky or something. The person who had passed away was usually still in bed, and that's where I had to do most of my measuring up. Over the years I've visited many places doing this. The coffin was usually delivered to the house and the body stayed in the house with the lid off until the day of the funeral, when it was screwed down. Funerals were always sooner after a death than now.

One day, about twelve months after I started, I was working at the boss's house at Cloud Farm, up the Doone Valley. A decorator had come up there and we were talking about wages. He said, "What do you get a week?" and I said, "Seven and six." "Is that all you get?" he said, "You should get more than that! Why don't you join the trade union?" Well I hadn't heard much about a trade union, really. Anyway, he persuaded me and the following time he came up he brought some forms for me to become a member, which I did. And the following week I got a pound and a penny for my week's work – almost three times as much! Mr Nancekivell wasn't too happy about it. "No need for you to have joined the trade union," he said, "I would have put your wages up without that." Do you think he would have? It was then, when my wages went up, that I started saving for a motorbike.

*Victor on the left and Margaret, whom he married,
with her brother George on Countisbury Hill.*

I was seventeen when I got the first one, a second-hand Royal Enfield, and, do you know, it had gas lights! I bought it off one of the farm labourers who worked up at Oaremead. That was a proud moment; I can still remember riding it home up from Brendon to Cross Gate that first time. You didn't have tests back then, you just set off! Petrol was rationed – I've still got my old ration book and identity card somewhere – but for some reason we didn't have much of a problem getting petrol here. There were pumps down at the Rockford, one at the Staghunters, one at Barbrook, another at Countisbury at the Blue Ball – they were everywhere, not like now.

We were lucky living on a farm during the war because we were never really short of much at all. We were almost completely self-sufficient for food, although we never had much fruit, oranges or bananas or such, but we had most other things. There wasn't much official meat either, but we could always fix that, living in the country.

The war finished when I was eighteen. I remember there was a big do down at Lynton, a celebration in the area between the Valley of Rocks hotel and the church – a band playing, and drinking and dancing. There were huge numbers of people there.

Then Margaret Graham and I were engaged. She was from Wilsham, the farm to the north of Cranscombe, on the other side of the valley. You can see the Wilsham fields from the front of

Cranscombe, and we used to call right across the valley to the Grahams, who were working a good mile away in their fields, and have conversations with them, a sort of yodelled conversation, going backwards and forwards across the valley high above Rockford. We always used to call over to Farmer Graham whenever we had a ewe with a breached lamb. He had a very small delicate hand and could easily straighten out unborn lambs inside a ewe. That was in the days before people had telephones!

I left Cranscombe when I married; I was the first of our family to leave Cranscombe. My new wife and I decided to go to live in Bridgwater, where I had an aunt. We'd been up there a couple of times before she was my wife, and she quite liked it up that way. There was also work there; not that there was any shortage of it in Lynton at that time. In fact Mr Nancekivell, my old boss, didn't want me to leave Lynton. But in the end my wife wanted to come away so we did.

We'd go back to Cranscombe practically every other weekend, to visit both our families, first on the motorbike and then later in the car when we got one. Life in Bridgwater was different in every way from the life we had at Cranscombe. It was all a bit of a shock, the moving, with everything so different, but I came through it.

Interviewed January 2008

Blanche (née Watts) and John Pile

John was born at Hallslake, a farm between Brendon and Hillsford Bridge, in 1921, and remained there for the next seventy years. He met wife-to-be Blanche Watts at one of the dances during the war. "There used to be blackout curtains across the doors at the dances, and all of a sudden couples would disappear round those black curtains – ourselves included!" Blanche was from Manor Farm up on the Ilkerton Ridge, between Barbrook and the Chains, and she was five years younger than John. They were married in 1947. John retired in 1992 and they moved into a cottage a stone's throw from Manor Farm, Blanche's birthplace.

MY MOTHER WAS Evelyn Perkins and she was born up at Slocomslade, above Brendon. She used to walk to Brendon School from there, three miles each way I think it was, and with a big climb too. She would stop off on the way back and watch John Floyd the woodcarver in his workshop opposite Oaklands. She told me that there was often a little group of kids standing at the open door, watching him work. They'd almost always stop there until he got fed up with them and sent them on their way.

Her mum, my Grandma Perkins, was from Rockford and my Great-Grandma Sloley was from Rockford too, and she used to deliver all the babies in the area; she was the local midwife. I don't know how it all started, perhaps at that time if they were interested they just took it on. Probably she learnt through doing it.

She used to arrive at the house where a baby was due with all the things she needed in a basket, and the children in the house were always told that their new brother or sister would be coming in this very basket. That's where they thought all babies came from in those days: Great-Grandma Sloley's basket!

This is one of the earliest pictures we have, and is on a glass plate. Great-Grandma Sloley is in the middle, holding the child. She delivered all the babies in Rockford, and my Grandma Perkins is on the left of the picture, with her family round her. It must have been taken somewhere in Rockford in the 1890s or 1900s.

At that time it was the custom after a birth to bind the navel of a newborn baby tightly with a coin. Great Grandma Sloley would put a half crown on, and bandage it in. This she did one time up at Shilstone Cottages, and when she went back the next day there was a penny there! I remember mother saying that the man living there was a good man, but his wife was a bit the other way round, and she must have had the half crown!

Father's name was Charles Watts and his mum, my Granny Watts, was a Delbridge. Her people were the wheelwrights at Barbrook.

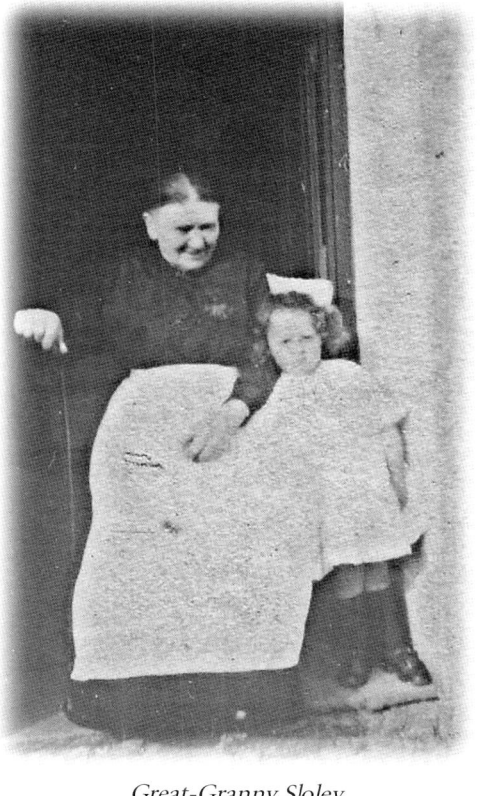

Great-Granny Sloley

They worked from Forge Cottage, which is still there; the flood destroyed the forge but the cottage survived. One of Father's aunts, Jane, started a school in one of the rooms at Forge Cottage; she ran what was called a dame school there. This was before the Barbrook school was built.* She wasn't very well and that's what she did.

Granny Watts and her sister were wonderful seamstresses and in their younger days they would travel from place to place, set themselves up, and do all the sewing for the family they were with. They took all they needed with them, and, depending on what they were doing, Granny would often take her dressmaking machine along in a cart and set it up for the few days at the place they were staying. It was

---

* Barbrook was originally known as Barbrook Mill. The Methodists built and ran the school, which opened in 1872 and finally closed in 1967.

a beautiful old cast-iron treadle machine and years later I inherited it. I wish I still had it.

Whatever was needed, they would make; I don't know about curtains and cushions, but certainly all the bedding items, and of course all the clothes. She made almost everything I owned when I was little, for example. I don't know if she had any patterns, but she certainly used to do copying. People would have something that was completely worn out, unrepairable, and they'd want the same again, and that's what she'd do. Much of her work was mending: turning sheet sides into the middle, turning worn-out collars back to front, putting patches on elbows, that sort of thing. She always had a tin full of buttons that she'd had off things, and I can remember as a child loving going through that tin. If she wasn't at her machine she still kept herself busy. I remember she always had little pieces of quilting she'd be getting on with at odd moments – except on a Sunday, when you never did a lot of work as far as she was concerned. She was a big churchgoer, and I used to walk down to Barbrook Church each Sunday with my Granny Watts. She and I were very close and we used to talk together a lot.

Granny Watts and Mum and myself outside Manor Farm.

JOHN: Grandma Watts had been to Hallslake before we lived there, sewing for the Cricks who were there at that time. She and her sister had done all the mending in a room with a big black stove and a door at the back which led directly out on to the splat. When she came up there after we married she would always say of the farm, "This aint like it used to be!"

Barbrook School in about 1904.
Dad, Charles Watts, is third from the right in the front row.

BLANCHE: Dad was born and grew up at South Stock, and he used to walk down from there to Barbrook School, which he started at in the very early 1900s. They say that there were about seventy children there at that time, with two teachers, Mr Hardman the headmaster and his assistant teacher. There was only one room at the school at that time and all the teaching was done in this one room to all the different age groups.

My mum was at East Ilkerton Farm before she married and used to take the milk down from the farm to Lynton in fair-sized churns in the back of a pony trap. The churns then were made of metal, with brass bands round; they did look beautiful, those old churns. I think she did deliveries from house to house down there.

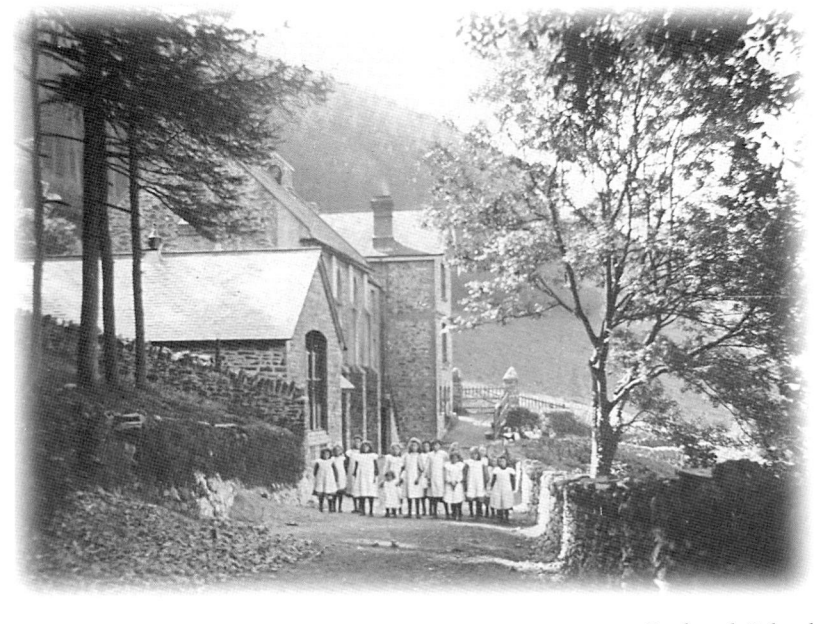

Barbrook School.

I grew up at Manor Farm, which is where both my parents and my grandparents before them farmed. We used to take in summer visitors, and many of the early photographs we have were taken by these visitors, who sent copies back to us. We would advertise in *Dalton's Weekly* but most people came through word of mouth.

Granfer and Granny Watts at Manor Farm (Philip and Alice Watts).

Visitors to Manor Farm would send back copies of their pictures.

It was a lovely childhood for me and my brother Philip, growing up at Manor Farm. We were surrounded by animals, not just farm animals but we had pets too, and we both learnt to ride at an early age. The holidaymakers who came year after year used to take us out with them on their day-trips. We were very lucky.

Another picture which arrived in the post, of myself with one of our summer visitors.

27

We'd just catch a horse anywhere in a field and jump on!

One of our favourite places to play on the farm was down by the river and you'd often find us there. We used a fallen tree as a bridge over the river to our uncle's farm next door, where we were always visiting. If the weather was bad we'd play indoors with table skittles or bagatelle. I loved doing jigsaw puzzles.

There was an endless stream of relatives visiting the farm. My Grandma's people were from Bristol and the easiest way for them to visit was on the paddle-steamers which stopped at Lynmouth. We'd go down when the steamer arrived and watch all the passengers getting into little rowing boats and being rowed ashore. Besides the relatives and the holidaymakers, we had all the delivery carts, and later the vans coming to Manor Farm. The baker from Lynmouth used to deliver on a horse and cart. He was called Herbert and, I don't know why, but I was the favourite and always got a bun off him. He used to come three times a week. Another regular delivery was from Burton Stores, with all our groceries. They used to be where the leather shop is now in Lynton, up near the bank.

Brother Philip at Lynmouth beach with one of the families who were staying with us.

We had an orchard at Manor Farm and we spent a lot of time in there as kids. Many of the trees were old varieties, even then. We didn't plant it, it was well established when my grandparents took it over. We used to give the apples away, feed them to the sheep; we'd never make cider.

*My dad on the top and the two grandfathers
carrying hay at Manor Farm.*

When I got older, in my early teens, I used to go into Lynton to do the shopping. I was coming back along the narrow lane one time when I heard a terrible scraping noise. I had the presence of mind to go back to where the road was wider. Almost immediately, a runaway

*Myself with a visitor and Roy the dog. Wherever I went, so did Roy.
The hay was always gathered into pooks before it was pitched on to the cart,
and there we are leaning against one, with the others in the background.*

horse with a cart on its side came tearing down the hill. Something had spooked it and it had bolted. If I hadn't gone back to a wider part of the road I'd certainly have been crushed. When I got home my grandfather was crying: he knew the tearaway cart was going down the lane and that I was coming up, and there was nothing he could do. That was the only time I had seen him cry, either before or afterwards.

My grandfather Philip Watts at Manor Farm on his favourite horse, Black Bess. He was a Lynton Town Councillor for many years.

One of the local characters at that time was an old chap that everyone called Neighbour Hoyles. He lived on the way down to Barbrook, and as a child I'd often drop in and have a chat. He used to go out on the railway line snaring rabbits – he wasn't meant to be there – and one time he was caught taking a rabbit from one of his wires. "I was just up here going fer a walk," he said, "and I heard this little rabbit shouting, 'Hoyles, let me out, let me out!' and I just had to let the poor little thing out!" he said. What happened to old Neighbour Hoyles, whether they let him off, I'm not sure!

I went to Barbrook School myself in 1931. By this time they had built an additional classroom on the side and the infants were in there with one teacher, and the older ones were in the second classroom. Miss Kippling was my teacher. She used to live in one of the

On our way to school with my two cousins
Jack and Bert Jones.

Cherry Bridge Cottages immediately above where the petrol station is now
in Barbrook. It was just above here that I met the runaway horse.

cottages at Cherry Bridge. In those days there were three cottages and hers had one room up and one down. She lived in the bottom one, I remember.

It was a Methodist school but they didn't really try to convert you. We'd take part in the Harvest Festivals and Methodist anniversaries and things like that because the chapel was all part of the school, but otherwise it was just a normal school.

When I first started there was no sports or games because the school didn't have a playground, which also made lunch-times and breaks a bit difficult. We had to try to play on the steep hillside next to the school. It was ever so slippery there, you could hardly stand up. The boys used to toboggan down the slippery grass on sheets of tin they got from the dump. That's how we spent the lunch break before the playground was built. Well, one time there was almost a terrible accident when a cousin of mine tobogganed out into the road and a teacher called Miss James almost ran him over in her new car. She wasn't pleased and that put a stop to the tobogganing!

The opening ceremony for the new playground at Barbrook School.

Soon after this Captain Slater gave a bit of land to the school and the playground was built. I was involved in a little opening ceremony – I'm in the circle of children there in the photograph – and after that we had tennis and other organised games.

We studied most things. We always had Scripture in the morning, first thing, and then the three Rs. The girls had sewing classes and we all had dance, a sort of folk-type dance class. School was free – Dad didn't have to pay anything for us to go. I'll always remember sitting in afternoon lessons and seeing the narrow-gauge railway train from Barnstaple going along the opposite side of the valley as it made its way to Lynton.

This is my school photograph. We all stood in front of a canvas scene, one by one. I liked school so I've got to say I think it was a good school. Others didn't like it. Jim Sanders didn't

The first fatal car accident in the area was at the bottom of the old Beggar's Roost road next to the school. This resulted in the new road being built, up past where the pub is now.

like the school and was always being punished. One time he was put out in the cloakroom as a punishment and the next thing we all knew he was up the road going home. My brother was a bit like that too!

The old Beggar's Roost road used to go steeply up beside the school to the top and it was very dangerous for the early motor cars when they started arriving in the area. After a fatal accident on that hill the Council started to build the current road in a gentle sweep up to the Beggar's Roost pub, where it rejoined the old road at the second hairpin bend at the top there. Two of my mother's brothers carted road chippings with a horse and butt and were involved in the building of the new road.[*]

The old road continued to be used for motor trials, and in fact we had visitors coming year after year to stay at Manor Farm who'd come to the area specially for the Motorcycle Trials. We had room for six visitors but during the Trials they'd say, "Mrs Watts, if you can take more than six, we'll sleep anywhere!" And they did!

[*] The first motor car arrived in Lynton in 1901, having made its way along the terrible road from Minehead. Motor traffic to the area increased year by year and it is recorded that at Easter weekend in 1906 almost sixty cars had visited the town. Many could not make it up Lynmouth hill and had to be taken up on the cliff railway, the passenger carriage of which could be removed for taking up heavy loads. By 1906 four of the hotels had opened garages on their premises, as well as continuing to run their stables.

Mother prepared all the evening meals for the visitors, which were served in the dining room. The only midday meal she did was on a Sunday, and this was always roast chicken and junket. With the junket you had to add the rennet to the milk at blood-heat and we always made it immediately after milking, while the milk was still warm from the cow.

After a pig was killed everyone was expected to help. All the innards were removed and the liver cut into slices and fried. The intestines we as kids would take down to the river and wash out completely – which was a bit of a chore. Then they would be stuffed and hog's pudding was made with the small intestine, and two sorts of sausage were made from the bigger ones. One was stuffed with all the offal minced and added with a grain, a type of cereal called groats, and the other one was stuffed with any small pieces of meat. Both types were sewn up and then boiled, and hung up to dry off a bit. These were always called "pot-and-puddings". We also made tail-pie when the lamb's tails were docked, and cleaning up those tails I remember was another of our jobs – another slow, tedious job. Picking poultry was another. We'd save the feathers, the small ones, and the gipsy folks would buy those from us, and make pillows, probably, or mattresses.

John's great-grandmother Julia Pile, née Ridd, in about 1899 or 1900. John's dad David is on the left.

JOHN: Well, on my side of the family my great-grandmother was Julia Pile, and she was originally a Ridd. My father David was born in 1896 and we've got a picture of him and his mum taken when they were at East Lyn Farm. Later my grandparents took on Hallslake and moved, and that's how Father came to meet Mother, who was a Sanders from Shilstone – Mary Sanders. Her mother came from Brendon Barton, which was the neighbouring farm but one.

A sheep-shearing class organised at Kibsworthy.

In the early days each farmer would teach their own sons how to shear with the hand-held shears, but it seems they also used to organise shearing classes. We've got a picture of a shearing class held at Kibsworthy Farm and I think that father's in it – that's what I have been told – but I can't quite make it out because many of their heads are down.

At that time, and for years afterwards, in about June the farmers would go to all the other farms in their shearing circuit and help with the shearing. They then had a big party afterwards, eating, drinking and singing. Most of their families went along in the evenings and joined these parties, which were one of the most important social highlights of the year. The shearing and parties went on for weeks and weeks, until all the sheep in the whole area had been done and the wool was ready for sale. The wool cheque was always the biggest cheque on the farm. Hallslake used to join up with ten or eleven

*Granfer John Perkins
from Lower East Ilkington.*

other farms, so you can see how big these parties were, and the number of people that needed catering for at each farm.

All the women would be preparing the food and making arrangements for weeks before everybody arrived at each farm. Vast quantities of beer were also brewed for these shearing parties. In fact, most farms brewed beer all the year round, and I can remember father brewing his beer. He had the hops from somewhere Parracombe way, and the malt from Porlock. He had a whole lot of vats made of wood in one of the outhouses. He used to boil up the mixture in the furnace and then put it into these barrels to ferment. He'd brew three or four times a year, for the shearing, for Christmas, for birthdays and so on. He'd put water into some of the beer to make it weaker and more thirst-quenching, and that would be given out during the day as the men worked, and he'd have other vats which were stronger for the evenings. He always brewed at Hallslake, but didn't do it so much when he moved to Yenworthy. Then he started to use barrels of commercially made beer.

Father would always offer a drink to anyone arriving at the farm, no matter what time of day it was. Most of the farmers in the area would. He had a number of horn cups, and these he'd fill from the

*The shearers in their white suits at Yenworthy, which was one of the
ten farms or so on the shearing circuit with Hallslake.
Granfer Pile is in the centre with the trilby hat on.*

Grandfather bringing the sheep in.

tap at the bottom of the beer barrel and hand round. Well, we had an old shepherd called Abe Antell who looked after Father's sheep out on Cheriton Ridge. He lived miles from anywhere out at Hoar Oak with his wife Gert and he'd very often drop down to Hallslake, hoping for a drink and a bit of company. He'd always arrive with an excuse: he was short of a pony, he wanted to know something – you know – but he was really after a drink, which he always got. One time father thought he'd put Abe off a bit and lent him a pony to go home on, a wild old chestnut pony that hadn't been ridden for ages. Father thought Abe would have a bit of a game getting home, that the pony would have him off up on the common! I think it did, but Abe said nothing, and he still kept coming just the same!

We'd sometimes see him and his missus riding in to the Rockford pub, both on the same pony, one behind the other. They'd get a bit tipsy and then both ride all the way back again.

Sheep-dipping.

BLANCHE: Years before, Abe had been down to Manor, helping carry the hay, and Granfer had given him a small firkin, a little barrel made of wood with brass bands, full of cider. "I want that firkin back!" Granfer had said. Well, we all knew we'd never see it again and

Granny wasn't very pleased because she was going to have some new bands put on it. Well, years later, when we were living at Hallslake, Abe pitched up one time. He screwed up his nose and said to me, "I got something you want, aint I?" he said. "I'll bring it back one day!" A few weeks later he did just that, he brought it back all repaired with new brass bands. I've still got it! Hoar Oak is completely abandoned now, its just a shell of a building out on the common; the cattle have got in and knocked it about. Shame really.

John returning home from Brendon School with brothers and sisters and the Ash girls from Bridge Ball.

JOHN: As children we were expected to work, of course, to do jobs, both before going to school and when we got home. Some of my friends would go up to Scob Hill Gate after school and wait there for the cars to come along so they could open the gate and get a penny, but I had to go home and do my jobs.

We didn't have many toys as kids, really. I remember getting an apple and an orange for Christmas in our stocking, that sort of thing rather than toys. We always used to go outside to play if the weather was right and we'd get up to mischief out there. We had a cart — home-made with a piece of wood and four wheels, probably pram wheels, and we'd ride it down the slopes in the fields. Trouble was you couldn't turn the wheels, you couldn't steer, and each time you'd always go a little further up the hill to get more speed. One time I went straight into a stone wall in the hedge and cut my head. I went in, found Mother and said, "I've broke me neck!" Well, there was a labourer working there and he put me in a cart and took me down to Dr Head. The doctor fixed me up, he put in a couple of stitches!

There were eight of us kids in the family. I had an older sister, Rose, who was about eighteen months older than me, and then I followed and was the oldest boy. My brothers were George, Norman, Gerald, Donald, Raymond and Kenneth. They came every two years roughly, although there were some gaps because mother lost some of her babies. Three of us boys used to share a room. In fact three of us shared a double bed until we were quite big – a double bed with a feather mattress and feather pillows and a patchwork quilt.

We shared our clothes too, really, all us boys, because they were handed down one to the next, you know. We also shared the bath water, all eight of us! It was a tin bath in front of the fire on a Saturday night. Saturday nights were always bath nights and Mother would put all her pans and kettles over the fire, hanging on crooks, and heat up as much water as possible. Then the little ones she'd put in two at a time, one at each end, and us bigger ones would take it in turns. We'd all get a good scrubbing with Lifebuoy soap! Of course everyone wanted to go in first when the water was clean and warm, but mother was pretty strict: you did as you were told, so there was never too much clammer.

At Hallslake there used to be a pump which was over a slate trough, and that is where we got all our water from. It was right outside the back door and came from deep underground. The waste went down a gutter, and then down the mead I expect. There was a big grinding wheel for sharpening everything out there too.

The toilet was the other side of the yard, a little room next to the dog-house. You had to cross the yard to get to it. It was just a seat over a bucket, just one seat ...

BLANCHE: At Manor Farm we had two seats over the toilet, two different-sized holes in a piece of wood, one big one and a little one for the children. 'Twas very drafty!

JOHN: Then the bucket was tipped out in the garden somewhere. If we wanted to use the toilet in the night we'd use a chamber pot. Before we went to bed, though, we'd all have to go to the toilet; Mother would see that we all went one by one out into the freezing yard!

Granfer's spaniel sitting on the grindstone.

43

I remember each morning father used to do the breakfast and he'd have a big frying pan full of potatoes. Fried tetties was the main thing at breakfast! Sometimes there'd be things added, eggs or bacon, or laver* or something. Everyone would have a job to do while the tetties were frying. Mother would be doing the bedrooms or something, some of the kids would be feeding the cattle, some turning the handle and chopping the mangolds, others going round the young stock, some dealing with the horses, and so on. Then, when breakfast was ready, father'd blow the hunting horn to get us all in! We'd have breakfast and then off to school. We went to Brendon School, which wasn't very far at all from Hallslake. I was there the same time as Tom and Evelyn Lock from Cranscombe. I didn't like school at all.

Quite often we'd have fried laver with the tetties, and the laver we'd have to collect from the shore-line, below Wingate Wood. We'd ride the ponies down as far as we could get, tie 'em up to a tree and then go on down to the shore-line. We'd fill up the bags and carry them

Brendon School in about 1932. John is in the second row up, second from the left. Both Tom and Evelyn Lock from Cranscombe are in this picture, Tom in the back row, four along, and Evelyn in the third row up, and six along.

* Laver is an edible seaweed, pronounced 'layver' on Exmoor, which is collected from the shore-line when there is an 'r' in the month. It was commonly used in this area on its own on toast or, as above, fried for breakfast. In other parts of the country it was used in sauces, often to go with fish, or with marshland mutton. The Bristol Channel, with its high tidal range, is one of the very few places that it is still gathered commercially and about 400 pounds each week is sold from Butcher's Row in Barnstaple.

back home. Mum washed it mainly, got all the sand out. We'd have it often, more than twice a week, probably, when it was in season. My favourite, though, was always egg with the tetties!

BLANCHE: At our house we'd quite often just have bread and cream for breakfast, which we'd take straight off the pan. Mother would scald it in two-and-a-half-gallon pans and the cream would set on the surface. We'd scoop it off with our fingers, all nice and crusty and put it on a slice of soft fresh bread – fantastic! For our evening meals we ate a lot of rabbit – everyone did, and, depending what you did with a rabbit, you could feed up to four people with it. My favourite as a kid was fried rabbit, a little one cut up so it laid fairly flat and fried like that. You'd need to watch out for the bones, though. Rabbit was one of the commonest meals. It was cheap and you could always go out with a ferret and catch a rabbit quite easily. Almost everyone had ferrets on the farms in those days.

JOHN: There was a big woodworking place on the river between Rockford and Brendon called Oaklands and any wood we wanted sawing up at Hallslake we'd take down there. They had a big circular saw which ran off a water-wheel. We'd pull our own logs out of

Barton Woods with a horse and chain and then take them down to Oaklands and they'd turn them into gates or fence posts. Alf and Bert Floyd were there then, two brothers. Alf was the wheelwright and Bert did the general stuff. As a child I can remember going down and dropping off things for repair, and the whole place being full of implements and carts in various states which the farmers had left.

Further up in Brendon was the Richards' mill, which was another timber mill, but they also had a stone and did a little grinding. We used to take a couple of sacks of corn up there in a cart and wait while they ground it. The corn was for animals, not for our own consumption.

Blanche's father on his way to Blackmoor Gate with a visitor in the back.

We still had working field gutters up at Hallslake and continued to use them well into the time I took over. The water came down from a pond and we'd open the sides of the gutters to feed it out into the fields. We never added manure or anything to the water.

Blackmoor Gate was where the animal auctions were, and where most people went with their stock. Much of the stock for a long time was driven along what is now the A39.

Brendon Pony Sale, with John in a brown coat in the centre, holding a riding crop.

We had a good number of horses and ponies, breeding them and breaking them in, with plenty of Exmoor ponies, of course, out on the common. Father seldom missed the Brendon Pony Sale and we'd always take ponies to Bampton afterwards in a lorry, sometimes up to forty or even fifty ponies. Bampton was a wild carry-on and it was stopped in the end by the RSPCA. We used to lead the wild ponies up the street, one man at the front and the other at the tail, and that was said to be cruel. It wasn't a very convenient place to sell them anyway.

All our ponies we'd brand and set out on the common. With the sheep each farmer would leer their flock to a certain part of the common and that's roughly where he'd find them, but with the ponies it was different – they'd go anywhere.* There was no fences between here and Dunkery Beacon, and the ponies would roam as far as that. When we rounded up in those days, we'd meet up with the Porlock fellows and all go up to Dunkery. We'd bring the herds over this way, gradually parting out each farmer's stock as we passed his place. The ponies that gathered round the Porlock area were always in better condition than the ones that had lived in the wilder places. Father's brand was "DP", and you'd look for that on the ponies, and the suckers would follow their mothers so you knew which of the foals were yours too.

Once you'd got all your own ponies back home, you'd pick out the best ones to keep and the others you'd sell at the Brendon or Bampton pony fairs. You'd keep the good mares and get rid of all the male ponies. I continued with this when we took over Hallslake, the only difference being that the ponies didn't roam so far in my day because by then a lot of fences had been put up.

BLANCHE: There were a lot of tramps coming round the farms in those days. Quite a few were ex-servicemen from the first war. There was a shed in a field at Dean Steep, on the Caffyns side of Barbrook, which was called the Toc H Shed, and that's where they used to gather and spend the night. They'd be squabbling there, cooking there, and people were afraid of passing by, really, because of all the chaps there. It belonged to Granfer Jones and he would allow them to stay. The tramps all knew that the Toc H Shed was available and often went there instead of just going in someone's barn or outhouse.

JOHN: There were also quite a number of gipsies. A lane at the top of Beggar's Roost is called Gipsy Lane because that's where the travellers used to stop with their caravans. They used to make their camps there. During the forties I remember there was a travelling family called Birch who would stay for quite a long time. They'd pitch up and stay, making spar-gads for thatching and wooden clothes pegs.

During the war years the main thing I did was to clear the common before the rocket firing started. Father and I would both do it;

---

* Each time the farmer took his sheep to the common he'd take them to the same place and the sheep would gradually learn to associate this as their home patch and would naturally stay in that area, or return to it. Farms were often sold with sheep that had been leered to nearby common. Deer, too, are leered to the part of the common in which they were born, and to which they return.

I had the Cheriton Ridge and father would do the Hawcombe and Badgworthy area of Brendon Common. Jack Edwards was in charge and used to come up and tell us when the next firing was due to start. Sometimes we'd have to be up there at 5am, 6am, that sort of time, and we'd get the whole place cleared of stock. We'd set off on a pony with a good dog. 'Twas

mainly Exmoor ponies at that time on Cheriton Ridge. I'd go up to the upper end and drive them all back towards the farm and try to calm them down there until the firing started. Of course when the firing did start they stayed back of their own accord! We were paid by the government each time we cleared the common, and I think I spent all my share at the dances!

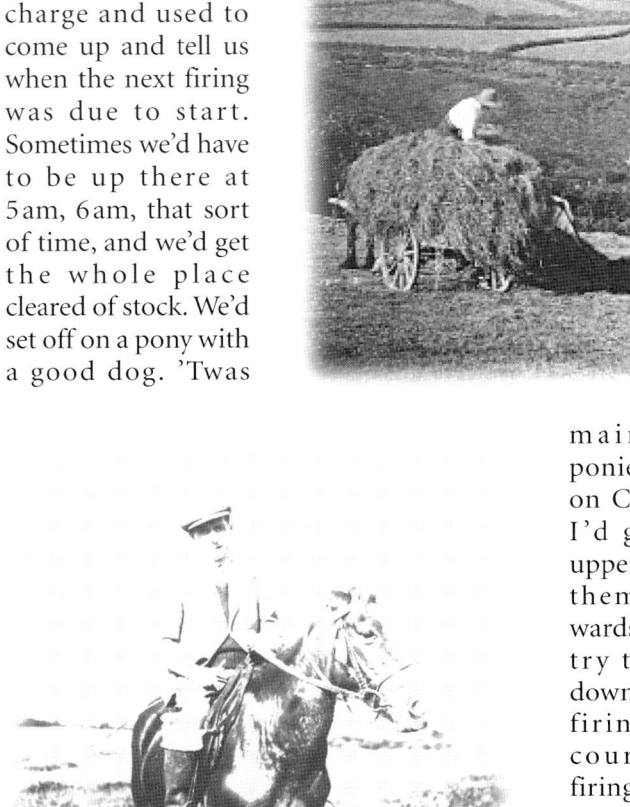

The annual dinner/dance for the Brendon Home Guard at the Staghunters.
Some of the Porlock Home Guard are there too.

Notices went up warning people, and Jack would also go round various farms telling them not to go on the common at such-and-such a time. It would mostly have been only shepherds out on the common then. Whether the shepherds did some of the clearing too, I'm not sure. It was cement posts that the Army were aiming at; I think cement posts were the targets.

Besides clearing the common, I was also in the Home Guard, where Major Taylor was in charge. We used to have a dinner/dance each year at the Staghunters which was organised by my Aunty Connie, who did all the bookings down there. In the photograph I'm the one standing on the extreme left.

We didn't have much to do with the Americans at Hallslake. They were in a big camp up at Cross Gate, and there was another camp in the field opposite Brendon Manor. I think Father was paid for the use of that field after they'd all cleared out. It was a terrible mess after all the heavy vehicles had been in it.

BLANCHE: We had an evacuee staying with us very briefly, a little boy. Mum had a cousin in London who rang up and asked if a friend's little boy could be evacuated to us, a lad of about four and a half. Well Mum thought about it and said it were better to have

Stewart the evacuee and his mum.

someone like that than someone we didn't know at all, so we agreed, and Stewart came. He arrived on the train with his mother. Well, he soon wandered about as if he owned the place! Then after a few weeks he fell ill and his mother wanted him back. That was the end of our experiences of evacuees and the last we heard of Stewart!

John and I were married at Lynton in 1947, and we had the reception up at Manor Farm. Mum's sisters and I did all the catering. Mum and I made the wedding cake in an old black Bodley stove. We'd read somewhere that if you put the cake tin on a tray of salt that would reduce the heat in the oven to the right temperature, and it worked a treat. Then I set about icing the cake and it was the first time I'd iced anything in my life. It turned out reasonably well! We borrowed a cake stand from the baker.

JOHN: We took over Hallslake from Father and he went on to Yen-worthy. Hallslake was a mixed-stock farm of 230 acres, which rose from about 800 feet to over a thousand feet up near Scob Hill Gate.

John with one of the last heavy horses which he used for breeding.

I did a lot of breaking-in of horses and ponies. That was my main interest. Some would be brought in by people who wanted them breaking-in, others would just be off the common. Most of the work was done with another horse, a big steady horse was best. First you'd catch the horse you wanted to break and put a halter on. You'd drive him into the shed and push the quiet one up against him until you could slip the halter on. Then you'd lead him around outside. Depending on the horse, you might need two or three men on the halter at first. You mustn't break his spirit – it's essential you don't do that; you've got to get him to trust you. Sometimes you'd tempt him with something to eat, build up his confidence, play with him. Then you gradually put weight on his back; you begin to lean on him, little by little; show him you're not going to hurt him. Then you get a saddle and bridle on to him and tie him to a quiet horse, and finally you get on. Once you're on, the quiet horse restricts his movements a lot. Then you take him out riding regularly, every day if you can. The whole thing could take twelve months. I did it more for the interest than the money. I used to like horses.

Hallslake.

BLANCHE: When we went to Hallslake I did all the cooking for John and two of his brothers, who were with us most of the time. We had a solid-fuel stove put into the fireplace for me to cook on. We continued to cut the turfs out on the common every May, which we put into burrows out there to dry. We burnt a combination of these with sticks in the Rayburn. In the end we stopped cutting turf because it was very hard work; it was a lot easier to cut and split firewood and gradually that's what happened.

We had a small milking herd but didn't sell any milk and turned it to cream mostly, which I did each day. The milk was brought into the diary and we'd strain it through a piece of cloth. Then you'd leave it on a slate shelf for the head to come up. Next day you'd put it on the stove and scald it and then leave it again for the cream to set. We'd take the cream off with a skimmer, a flat round scoop like a ladle with holes, and put the cream into tins.

JOHN: Each morning I'd ride down to Hillsford Bridge with the cream and meet Mr Molland, who was going down to Lynmouth on his milk delivery. He'd take it down to the Nelson Tea Gardens who always had our cream for their cream teas.

53

BLANCHE: Then Mr Molland would bring the empty cream tins back each day and leave them next to the post box on the bridge at Hillsford, and John would collect them from there when he passed by.

JOHN: Brendon School always had Sports Day in one of our fields, Straypark it was called, between the school and the church. We kept all the sports equipment at Hallslake for years – ropes, high jumps and all the other equipment.* We also ran the autumn livestock sale there once a year from the same field, and Dobbs the livestock auctioneer from South Molton would come. That was in the days when farmers drove their stock to auction. It would never work now with all the big lorries in those narrow lanes.

BLANCHE: Then in the early fifties Mother and Father got one of the new televisions up at Manor Farm. They had good reception, which came from Wales. We used to make special trips over to Manor Farm to watch telly, especially the show jumping. One time we saw reindeer for the first time on the box. We all knew what red deer looked like and were fascinated to see the reindeer. We talked about it for days afterwards, I remember.

JOHN: If one household had a telly in those days, all the relatives would be round watching it. When the programmes got more interesting that's what people did. Gradually all the get-togethers – with people playing cards and singing and talking – gradually that all stopped. The get-togethers for the shearing continued a while, but the rest began to dwindle away.

BLANCHE: It was about this time that our children were born. We had two daughters and a son. Mary was born in 1951, Anne in '54 and our son Philip in '57. When they were little I used to help with the lambing, which was hard work, especially when you had to look after three children at the same time. I remember taking the kids across the fields, one running alongside me, one on my shoulders and the other in a push-chair, and trying to keep an eye on them and do the lambing. I'd put them outside the wire as I worked.

---

* The Brendon School Sports Day and the Harvest Home had adults as well as children participating in many of the activities, which included cross-country races and tug-o'-war.

Mary, Philip and Anne.

JOHN: Sheep and wool were always a big part of the farm. In Father's day everyone sheared with hand-clippers. Then mechanical shears came gradually in. The first mechanical clippers worked on a fly-wheel which had to be turned by hand. There was a set of these at Manor Farm…

BLANCHE: … And I can remember turning them. You had to keep it going very steady.

JOHN: Then came clippers fitted to a diesel engine, but they made a terrible rattle in the barn and drove you mad. Finally came the electric shears, and with them the contract shearers who went from farm to farm. You'd pay them by the number of sheep sheared. There was a counter on the clippers which they'd flip every time a sheep was done. When he grew up, our son Philip became a contract shearer. He worked our farm at Hallslake all year except for shearing time, when he went round the other farms.

With the wool, we'd tie each fleece with string in the early days and fling them into what we called the wool-chamber in the back of the

John and son Philip in the barn at shearing time.

barn.* Then a chap would come round and grade it by pulling out just a few fibres. He was called Mr Quance and was from South Molton. Exmoor Horn always got the best prices. He'd then weigh all the fleeces with a set of weights which he'd

Philip at Brendon Barton with Dick French

* An extremely memorable description of the tied fleeces comes from country writer Dorothy Hartley: "The fleeces were still live and warm [and] if the summer night was cold after a hot day, a mist, like the bloom on a fruit, clouded the wool, and the cooling fleeces stirred slightly all night through. Most live materials have tension. The fibres of wool, in tension, are locked together like the plumes of a bird's feather, and in the old wool-room you could hear the fleeces stirring; a faint sound like soft breathing."

56

Blanche's brother Philip with the wool sacks.

brought with him. A lot of the farmers had their own weights, but he wouldn't trust them. He'd pull up beside the barn, sling all the fleeces into the back of the lorry, and then set off to the next farm.

In later years we didn't have to tie up each fleece. We'd get a huge sack from the Wool Marketing Board and tie these sacks up with ropes from the beams of the barn, with the tops open. We'd fling each fleece into these until they were full, and then we stacked them all up to wait for collection. By this time there were all sorts of different grades and it got complicated. Then gradually the price of wool went down as people bought synthetic instead of real, and after a while you'd pay the shearers more than you got for the wool. And when that happened there was no point keeping sheep for the wool. That was the end.

Interviewed June, 2009

Philip Pile, 1957-1991

Ted Lethaby

Ted was born in 1925 at Top Cottage at Wilsham, the farm to the north of Rockford. In 1952 he married the lighthouse keeper's daughter, Barbara Roberts, and they moved into the old schoolhouse at Countisbury. His new home was a couple of miles from where he had been born and he's still there sixty years later.

All his life Ted has been closely associated with Countisbury Church. His father was the Sexton there, and it was where he was christened and married, and where all his family are buried. He likes living right beside it. "I can keep an eye on things, and they won't have far to carry me when the time comes!"

M Y GRANDMOTHER Jane Lethaby was born in 1848 and lived at Combe Foot, in the valley between Rockford and Brendon, and she was the baker and grocer there. According to the records, she was head of the household; there was no man about.

The bakery had an oven that was big enough to walk into. It was like a room in itself, and they'd put wood into it and light a fire and stoke it up until it was hot enough. Then they'd pull all the ashes out and put the bread in to bake. I don't know if the locals used to take their own meat and cakes there for roasting too, but I do know this used to happen in Porlock. On Christmas Day, for example, people used to take their turkeys into Stenners the bakers at Porlock for cooking, even in recent years.

Then when Grandmother died my Uncle Frank took over and ran the shop at Combe Foot. It was a grocer's shop selling essentials and it was small, like a little scullery really. The Kellaways in Brendon were also bakers, and I can remember Olive Kellaway delivering bread to Wilsham on a pony with a huge sack over her knees bulging out on each side with loaves of bread!

Mum originally married Dad's brother, and they lived at Top Cottage at Wilsham and had seven children. Then in 1915 Dad's brother died, leaving Mum to bring up all the children alone. The youngest was only eighteen months when this happened. I think this is when she started taking in washing from Glenthorne* – there was no social security then. She'd do all their washing, the ironing and starching too, the shirt collars and everything, and it all had to be spot-on for Glenthorne – she used to say if it wasn't right they'd send it back. I think she was washing most days then, full-time almost. She had started boiling washing long before I was born and was still at it well after I'd left school in 1939 – she'd been doing it all that time. She was a gentle lady always. I never saw her get upset, she was never drunk, she never smoked, and she never swore. I always said she was a model person. She would help anyone. She never needed to leave her cottage and I don't think she did really – maybe to go to Barnstaple once a year. Everything was delivered round the outlying places in those days, every last thing.

---

* Glenthorne was where the Halliday family lived, at that time owners of all the parish of Countisbury.

Ted's father Harry Lethaby, soldier, market gardener, stone-cracker, lengthman and Sexton.

Dad was in the Army, and when he left he married Mum and then they had two children, my brother Wilfred, who was born in 1922, and then three years later I was born.

On leaving the Army Dad went to work at Doone Cottage in Rockford as gardener for Mr Turner,* and he also grew vegetables himself – cabbages, beans, that sort of thing. People in Lynmouth used to come up to buy produce off him. Then he started working for the Council as a stone-cracker, breaking stones up at Scob Hill quarry. You can still see the quarry on the left on the Simonsbath road, before you get to the cattle grid there at the start of the common. In the morning his mate Bert Palmer would walk from Dewcombe to Wilsham, then he and Dad would walk together down to Rockford and up to Scob Hill quarry. That's a good hour's walk from start to finish – at the beginning and the end of a hard working day, too, and with steep climbs! He'd break stones to the size needed for the hardening in the roads. He'd start with a sledgehammer and break the big ones down, and then a good heavy hammer to break them down smaller until they were the right size. They used to wear gauze

* When Mr Turner died, Mr Bland lived at Doone Cottage. He was a retired policeman from Zanzibar and had plenty of money. Ted remembers him spending £5 on fireworks – a large sum then – and having a huge fire and letting the fireworks off one Guy Fawkes night. This was the first time Ted had seen fireworks.

glasses to protect their eyes; they were only small glasses with a very fine wire mesh to stop any flying chips of stone. He used to spend his time peering through those. Then, after the stone-cracking, he got a job as lengthman, doing all the gutters, cutting hedges, potholes, that sort of thing, along the road from Brendon Barton to Tippacott. Lengthmen were responsible for a certain length of road; for example, the chap at Wilsham, Fred Steer, used to do the road from Lynmouth to County Gate; that was his patch. The roads were very good then because each man took a pride in his own length of road.

The cottage at Wilsham had three bedrooms upstairs, and downstairs a sitting room, dining room and kitchen. The place was very cold because you didn't have Rayburns in those days; there was only an old open fireplace which mother'd have to come down in the mornings and stoke. She used a primus stove first thing to boil water on until the fire got going. Of course there was no running water then and nowhere to take the dirty water. You'd throw that into a slops bucket and then you'd carry it up the steps into the garden to the dung heap. That's where you threw everything, you know – all your potato peelings, greens, all your rubbish, everything. To fetch fresh water you had to go down the steps to the well, a scoop well. It had a little wooden door over the top and the water was underneath, and you'd dip your bucket into it.

The toilet was up the garden, up the steps at the back of the house, and it was a bucket too. When it was full it was chucked on to the dung heap as well. Out the back there was another shed and that's where the boiler was, where Mum did the laundry, and of course that was another fire she'd have to get going.

By the time I was born she'd cut down a bit on the washing, and was only doing it for Mrs Tattersall at Brendon Barton and Mr Read, who had the old farmhouse at Wilsham. The grocer Jack Bosson would travel round the farms delivering groceries, and he'd collect the dirty washing from the Barton as he did his round, and return it when it was done.

On washing day she'd have to get the fire going and boil and scrub all that washing, mangle it, put it through the rinsing water with the "blue", through the mangle again, and then hang it all up to dry! We didn't have a warm kitchen or anything to hang it in at night, so we'd hang it up at Mr Read's, who had a big open garage which was under cover. Drying it was the hard part; you get this sort of damp weather and there isn't much drying even indoors is there?

Brother Wilf and myself in the late 1920s.

Mr Read was an Oxford don and he came down for all his holidays. Mum used to do the cooking and cleaning for him and was his housekeeper when he was here, and Dad did the garden. He wasn't married, and he used to walk and read, and when he walked I remember he carried his stick horizontally behind him, wedged between his back and his elbows. Every Sunday he used to walk to Combe Park and have tea with the Vicar, a fellow called Jenkins, and the two Miss Buds who lived there. Mr Read was very vague;

one time he passed my mum on the bridge at Rockford and didn't even recognise her, even though she was in his house every day!

Wilsham farm itself took in visitors and I got to know their kids. They always used to come and greet me, you know, when they arrived. They also played interesting games; local kids would just mess about in the fields or the barns but these visiting kids would play charades, murder games ... they introduced interesting games.

The children who stayed at the farmhouse played interesting games.

Mr Read always brought a man called Leslie Franks down. I don't know where he fitted into the equation really – quite a young boy he was, at first. Then he used to drive Mr Read around in a little MG, a little sports car; he became Mr Read's chauffeur. Then when Mr Read died Leslie Franks took on the old farmhouse himself and came down with Mrs Franks, who was a fairly well-to-do person. He became an Alderman in Oxford I think.

I went to Countisbury School and used to walk there – about a mile and a half. I'd collect the teacher's milk on the way in a can from Combe. I used to walk up Wilsham and across the common because it wasn't ploughed up then – it was a gorse moor – down the lane into Coombe Farm, pick up the milk, then up over one field, two fields, down through the garden, across a little bridge and into school! The milk can I'd take back in the evening.

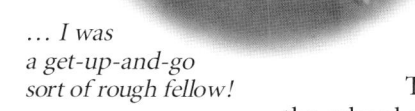

Mrs Beck and her daughter Miss Beck* were the teachers and they were very strict. If you did something wrong you'd always get into trouble – even on days off or in the holidays and they got to hear about it! I didn't like school very much because I was a get-up-and-go sort of rough fellow and I didn't like pen-pushing. I wasn't a very good speller, either. They used to have dictation every Friday morning and if you got seven mistakes you'd get the cane. Well, I used to hold my hand out for the cane before the dictation even started!

... I was a get-up-and-go sort of rough fellow!

There were two big tortoise stoves in the school and one was always lit in the winter. If you got wet going to school she'd say, "Stand beside the stove and dry off!" and that's really what I liked doing best at school – standing beside the hot tortoise!†

---

* Miss Beck spent her whole career at the school. She was a cherished and popular pillar of the community who married a local farmer, Mr Piercy, and on retirement received an MBE for her work at the school and in the community. Mr Beck, her father, was the local rat-catcher, now called an Environmental Health Inspector.

† Countisbury School replaced the old school at Countisbury (where Ted now lives) and was built because the original was too small, and perhaps too windy for the children's safety! W.H. Thornton, the Curate, taught there in 1854: "The wind blows so hard at the top of Countisbury Hill that I have, before now, waited for the children to leave, formed them into a string, and personally conducted them under the hill before I parted with them, fearing lest I should see some scholar going away to the height of a thousand feet, head foremost, towards Wales" Both of Ted's boys went to the new school, which itself closed in the early seventies. It later become a holiday let and Ben Halliday, the owner, remembers the band Deep Purple hiring it. He recalls seeing the band there, with their hair in pony tails and their guitars leaning up against the walls, and he apologised to them because the piano was out of tune, but they did not seem to mind. They were very polite and considerate, he says, and astounded him by calling him "Sir"! What they were working on is unknown. Ted remembers seeing them in the Staghunters.

I left school in 1939 and one Sunday in September George Graham* and I were on our way to pick laver in Wingate Wood, down below Desolate. On the way we dropped into Coombe Farm. It was eleven o'clock and the news came on the radio so we stopped and listened. It was Chamberlain telling us that war had been declared.

With the laver, you'd collect it on the shore-line and put it into bags and carry it back up to Wilsham – quite a climb, but we were young then; I was fourteen! You'd bring it up wet and then you'd start washing it, and that takes a lot of doing, the washing, especially if there's sand in it. Then you'd put it in a saucepan with vinegar and water and boil it up, and you'd add butter. We used to have it for breakfast with fried potatoes, or for lunch on toast – delicious! Years later I had an old twin-tub washing machine and I'd use that, and all the sand would sink to the bottom. You see, nowadays, when I buy it from the butcher's in Barnstaple, I've got to re-do it myself because it's not good enough. You've got to put butter and vinegar with it – they seem just to boil it up with water. They don't do it properly!

I'd quite often drop into the lighthouse on my way to gather laver on the shore-line down below Desolate.

---

* George Graham's father farmed Wilsham and George took the farm over when his dad retired. George and Ted were school mates and became life-long friends: "At our weddings he was my best man, and I was his." He died suddenly from a heart attack at the age of 49.

66

We used to get the laver down below Desolate, which is where Miss Darker lived. She was a character! She always had a scarf on, and a hat and a big coat, even in the height of the summer. She supposedly had a pilot's license – one of the first women pilots – and she used to look after all her vehicles herself out at Desolate, do all the mechanics and the maintenance herself. She was a bit of a loner, really. She used to get on very well with Mrs Beck and Mrs Piercy at the school and they used to go about together. She paid to have the electric taken out to Desolate there, underground – £4,000 it cost, which was a lot of money then.*

Ted during hay-harvest at Wilsham.

When I left school, the farm was the obvious place for me to work. All my life I'd lived next to it, and I'd always been involved with the farm and knew all about it; I hadn't got to learn anything new to start work. My brother Wilf was a carpenter and he had to cycle to the

* Indeed Miss Darker was a pilot, and the inspiration, it is said, for the navigator in *The English Patient*, written by her neighbour's brother at Glenthorne at that time, Michael Ondaatje. She was a mechanic and a keen cricket player, and in later life used to teach cricket to the children at Countisbury School on a fairly flat field belonging to Mr Onions at Coombe. This was after Ted had left the school himself. Desolate, where Miss Darker lived, was a small farm overlooking the Bristol Channel and tucked into a valley south of Desolation Point, after which it was named. Ted thinks it is no longer possible to get down to the sea there due to the lack of upkeep of the paths and slipways. Before Miss Darker lived at Desolate a Captain Keen had it.

other side of Barbrook to get to work, but working on the farm, I thought, I would just roll out of bed and I'd be there! So I started my first job when I was not quite fourteen, working for George's dad, Farmer Graham at Wilsham.

I used to milk the cows twice a day, seven days a week, and then do the milk-round down to Rockford. I hated milking! Half past seven each morning I'd have to get the cows in, and milk them by hand into buckets. You'd wash the udders first, but you'd still get a certain amount of dirt and hair in the milk, and this you'd have to strain out with a gauze, a sort of muslin which got any impurities out. Then you'd take the buckets into the dairy where Mrs Graham would have what she needed to make the cream and butter. What I wanted to take to Rockford I'd put into cans. I'd fill two milk cans which each held two and a half gallons. The lids had a little rim all the way round and I used to carry my measure-pots in this rim on the lids, and cream if anybody wanted cream. You weren't meant to sell cream in the war, but they used to call it "elephant's eggs"; they'd say, "I want some elephant's eggs tomorrow, please!" and I knew what they meant!*

Then I'd set off on the milk round, carrying my two cans. Out of the farmyard, across the fields, one, two, and then down that steep track and through the woods to Rockford. First place was the Youth Hostel, the buildings on the other side of the river from the Rockford pub. I'd measure out the milk into a jug which they'd left on the table for me. With most people I'd just go into their kitchens and fill their jugs, but at Green Tiles they used to leave their jug up by the gate, and at Alderford, the old boy who lived there, he used to leave his jug under the wall just down by the bridge, and he'd pick it up when he passed by later. Dr Head at Ferndale was one of my customers, and if I had a cold I'd mention this and he'd mix me up a bottle of tonic! I had ringworm once and he painted up the whole of my face with iodine. It worked!

Oaklands was as far as I went on the milk round. People didn't take much milk each day then; it didn't keep, not like today when you can keep milk for a fortnight. In hot thundery weather it would be a job to keep overnight without going off, and of course there were no fridges, so people had small amounts. In fact the Rockford, the pub,

---

* Cicely Cooper was the headmistress of Allerford School during the war years and attended meetings with local teachers at different schools in the area. She later said: "The teas grew tremendous. We all looked forward to going up into the hill country, where restrictions on cream did not seem to exist."

would sometimes come up to the farm to get fresh milk from the evening's milking if they thought that morning's milk wouldn't keep. It took me about an hour, an hour and a half, to finish the round. Then back to the farm and I'd wash out the buckets I'd used for the milking – just with cold water – and I'd turn them upside down on the wall to dry. There wasn't much hygiene then, but people didn't get ill, did they?

I'd collect the milk money once a week as I went round, but it never went to very much, a few shillings a week maybe. You always had trouble getting money out of some people, but most paid up. Tom Lock used to come down from Cranscombe with milk for various people – in fact there was a bit of rivalry between Cranscombe

milk and Wilsham milk! He took away one of my customers at one time. They said, "Cranscombe milk keeps longer than your milk!" and I said, "Yes, well water doesn't go off, does it?!"

Of course, between the morning milking and the evening milking I'd have to do all the other jobs on the farm. I worked at the farm for about twelve years, and when I gave it up to work on the buses it was partly so that I could have a day off once a week!

I joined the Home Guard on my seventeenth birthday because I couldn't join before. It was all local farmers and they were a fairly rough lot, but we took the training seriously! Major Tailor was the boss and he saw that we had plenty of equipment. The Sergeant Major was the chap who used to work at Wilsham with me, George

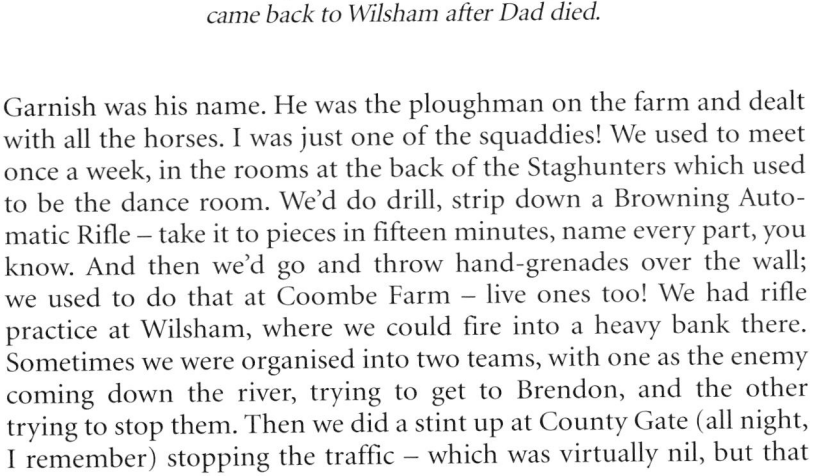

*Wilf's first car, an Austin 10, which he got when he
came back to Wilsham after Dad died.*

Garnish was his name. He was the ploughman on the farm and dealt
with all the horses. I was just one of the squaddies! We used to meet
once a week, in the rooms at the back of the Staghunters which used
to be the dance room. We'd do drill, strip down a Browning Automatic Rifle – take it to pieces in fifteen minutes, name every part, you
know. And then we'd go and throw hand-grenades over the wall;
we used to do that at Coombe Farm – live ones too! We had rifle
practice at Wilsham, where we could fire into a heavy bank there.
Sometimes we were organised into two teams, with one as the enemy
coming down the river, trying to get to Brendon, and the other
trying to stop them. Then we did a stint up at County Gate (all night,
I remember) stopping the traffic – which was virtually nil, but that
wasn't the point!

In 1947 I met Barbara. There used to be dances at Countisbury
School and that's where I met her. She was from the lighthouse on the
Foreland; she was the lighthouse keeper's daughter, and they lived in
one of the cottages there. I used to call her "the Gipsy" because her
dad was always moving to different lighthouses and the family never
settled anywhere for long. In fact, they'd already done a stint at the
Foreland once previously when she was a child and there was a
picture taken at that time of Barbara with a Kipscombe horse. The

farm all round the Foreland is called Kipscombe and it was farmed by the Hobbs at that time, Bill and Dave Hobbs.*

We were engaged on Derby Day, 1948 – and the horse that won that day was called "My Love", but I didn't have a bet on it! When her family returned to the Foreland Lighthouse the second time, her dad

Right: Barbara on the Foreland with one of the Kipscombe horses, and in the picture below she's second from the right in the front row in the Goodwick School band in 1938 – she always enjoyed her music!

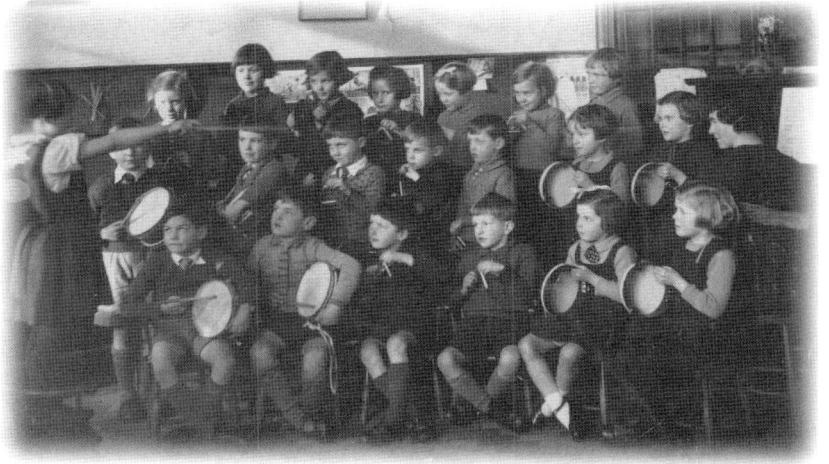

* Kipscombe is now owned by the National Trust, which bought up the whole of the Foreland and the cottages at the lighthouse – the only lighthouse on Exmoor.

71

was principal keeper. I used to walk down to the lighthouse from Wilsham, pick her up and then we'd walk on to Lynton to the pictures at the cinema there. *The Thirty-Nine Steps* with Jean Simmons I can remember going to – that was the sort of film which was on at the time.

This is the only picture I have of my mum,
second from the left, there at our wedding.

Some of the wedding guests outside the Blue Ball.

*The old school was built in 1835 and had been rented by
two old ladies before we bought it.*

We were married at Countisbury Church and then started looking for a place to live. Parts of the Glenthorne estate were beginning to be sold off at that time: Desolate was first, the Blue Ball pub was next, and then, third, was the old schoolhouse at Countisbury, by the gate to the church there. I tried to rent it but was told it was for sale only,

*My first car. It was grey until Barbara painted it black
one day when I was at work!"*

and to make them an offer. Dad said offer high if I really wanted it, so I offered £300. I've always said I could have had it for half that! Dad bought it in my name and I paid him 4% interest, which was £12 per year and like a rent, really. It was unusual for working people to buy their own houses at that time, but now of course I'm glad we did. It was a complete wreck and we named it Heathcliff, did it up and our sons Nigel and Jeremy were born there.

The Foreland Light-house was run by two men at that time, and of course Barbara and I spent quite a bit of time down there. The keepers used to do a four-hour watch between them; one man on and one man off, constantly alternating, twenty-four hours a day. The type of people who became keepers had to like their own company, really, and they had to be very independent and able to look after themselves. Often they were out on a rock for two months and had to do every-thing themself, cook their own bread even, you know – absolutely everything. They were self-sufficient and practical men, and that's what Barbara's dad was.

When they were on their watch they basically had to make sure the light was working at all times – that was their main job. They were supposed to do the watch from the service room, but actually they sat in their sitting room. Each seat in the sitting room had some method for seeing the light: this one had a little mirror rigged up which you could see the light in; from that one you could see the reflection of the light in the window, and from the one over there you could see

Barbara's dad in the sitting room at the Foreland Lighthouse
and (previous page), in his younger days with his assistant keeper.

the light on the white wall outside, and so on! They also had to do all the maintenance during their watches, fill up the oil lamps, clean the glass; there was yards of brass that wanted polishing, and so on.

The foghorn at the Foreland was a big gun rather than a horn, and it gave a bang every five minutes. The keepers had to get it going and keep it working when there was fog. It was clockwork and they'd have to go up and wind it and then make sure the caps were going through properly. It would jam regularly and they'd have to sort it out – it was a proper pain, that gun! They used to get 2d an hour extra for keeping the gun going when there was fog. Gun signals were uncommon but it was kept on here for years. Funnily enough, it didn't keep us awake at Countisbury. In fact, we couldn't hear it in our house because the lighthouse itself is set down under the hill from us. They could hear it in Lynton, though!*

When the Foreland became fully automatic in 1993, I started to help out with the lighthouse. The keeper at Bull Point used to look

---

* The lantern in the lighthouse was entirely enclosed by polished glass bull's-eye lenses. Measuring almost six feet across, the whole mechanism revolved (and thus flashed) by floating in a circular bath of quicksilver. Despite weighing four tons it was so delicately balanced that it could be set in motion with the pressure from a single finger. It was turned by clockwork weights on twenty foot chains and the lamp ran on vapourised paraffin, which was sprayed through a jet in the middle of the burner, where it mixed with air and burnt as a sootless flame, in exactly the same way as a primus stove works.

Barbara's grandfather and great-grandfather had both been lighthouse keepers, as well as her dad; it really did run in the family.

after this one too, and I was his second in command here. He lived at Bull Point, which was a man-and-wife station then, and he would call me when something needed doing over here. Years later he won the lottery – four or five balls and one bonus ball, I think it was – and he chucked his hand in with the keeping, bought himself a house in Barnstaple and died! Within the year, anyway, poor chap! Talk about terrible luck.

Ted with wife Barbara and Margaret Hoyles, landlady of the Blue Ball.

When I left the farm I started on the buses and I ended up doing the regular run from Lynmouth to Minehead, which connected with the London trains. My conductor was a man by the name of Jimmy Harris, an Irish fellow, and we were always on together. There were regular stops between Lynton and Porlock – in fact, we'd stop any-where at the side of the road if someone waved us down – but we were what was called the "express service" and then went straight through from Porlock to Minehead. There was just one run a day; we used to leave Lynton at quarter past nine, to catch the eleven o'clock train at Minehead, and then leave at quarter past four, having met the four o'clock train from London.

In the summer it was mostly visitors coming in on the railway and on a Saturday I'd always have to have at least one "dupe" – a duplicate bus – to meet the train because of the extra numbers of people travelling on Saturdays. They used to come for the week, staying at guesthouses or hotels, and Saturday was the change-over day. Youth Hostels were very popular then, too. Sometimes we'd need two dupes; in fact the record was one Saturday just before I started when they

needed thirteen coaches to come down to Lynmouth to take the people away! That shows how popular Lynton and Lynmouth was as a holiday destination at that time.

In the winter we still ran the service but there were fewer passengers – only locals, really, and it was quiet. We used to have regular locals, not every day, nobody went to work by bus every day, but we had once-a-week people who would go into the shops, see relatives, that sort of thing. It was an expensive run because it was the express run and that would have put some people off. There was also a lot of snow in those days in the winter and that caused some disruption to the service too.

Between the morning run and the afternoon run I'd sit in the depot in Minehead and play cards, or go out to the town, you know, look round. Sometimes they'd

Deep snow was very common in winters in those days.

put me on a run up to Taunton or somewhere – various places like that, short runs – but most of the time we'd just play cards until it was time to return. I was paid by the week, not just when I was driving. I'd started working on the buses in 1951 and left in 1954, and they were good days. I enjoyed my time on the buses.

On the night of the Lynmouth flood I was drinking with Ted Hoyles, the landlord of the Blue Ball, and we got a phone call from the Rising Sun down in Lynmouth saying that things were terrible down there. We jumped into Ted's old Post Office van, a green thing, and went down to the bottom of the hill, where we found complete mayhem, really. It was dark, pouring with rain, and the only time you saw anything was in the flashes of lightning which came regularly. We were there when the front corner of the Lyn Valley Hotel fell out. All the rooms had candles burning in them and we watched them blow out one by one. We couldn't do anything – there was no one else there on this side of the river, so we came back home again.

The normal routine in the morning was for me to go down to Lynton and pick up my bus. So, seven o'clock the next morning, I jumped on to the motorbike and went down, and that's when I took these photos, all from the bottom of Countisbury Hill. Of course I couldn't get anywhere near my bus, so I phoned the depot in Minehead from the Blue Ball and told them what had happened. They asked me to go into Minehead on the bike and fetch a bus from there. That is what I did, and drove the bus straight back.

The front corner of the Lyn Valley Hotel fell out. The rooms had candles burning in them and we watched them blow out one by one.

Meanwhile a lot of people had gathered at the bottom of Countisbury Hill. They were almost all holidaymakers from the small guest-houses and hotels on this side, up the Tors Road. There were a lot of people because it was August. Well, it was my job to get people to Minehead and the railway station there, and I knew I couldn't turn the bus at the bottom so I reversed all the way down Countisbury Hill, picked up a load of people and took them up to the top.

By now other buses had arrived at the top of Countisbury and they took the passengers from me, and back to Minehead. So I reversed down and got another load, drove them up, and there were still more people at the bottom so I reversed down again. I ended up doing that all day! It wasn't too bad reversing down Countisbury. The buses then didn't have the big wing mirrors like they've got now, so you did get it in the neck a bit.

The last load I picked up from Lynmouth were nearly all locals whose houses had been wrecked and they'd stayed till last, trying to sort things out. I picked them up and took them to Minehead, which was my normal route. When we arrived there they said, "What happens now?" and I said, "I don't know, I've brought you to Minehead – that's my job done!" Of course they really needed to get to Lynton because most of them knew people they could stay with at Lynton, which wasn't the case at Minehead. They got on to the Depot

Inspector and asked if they could all be got back to Lynton, taking a route that avoided Lynmouth. He said, "We can't do that, paying all that overtime to go right round!" So I said, "Look, if you don't charge them for going, I won't put in for overtime!" and he said, "All right then, take 'em!"

So another driver and I took two loads back to Lynton. It turned out to be about a hundred miles by the time we got there because all the bridges had been knocked out, and we kept on having to go in a bigger circle to try to get round. We got up to Exford and couldn't cross there, we couldn't get across the Bray Valley, and in the end we

went on to South Molton, then into Barnstaple and then round to Lynton. We arrived in Lynton at about ten o'clock at night, and I couldn't contact Barbara – all the phones were down and the Army with their walkie-talkies had all gone home. All I could do was sleep in the back of the bus, and I finally got home at about midday the following day, Sunday. Many weeks later I was the first bus back into town and I was greeted by the mayor!

One of the first bridges to go back over was built on two telegraph poles. The GPO had this photograph from me to use in their publicity.

I later had a little card booklet made up by Taylors, the photography people in Minehead, with copies of some of my photos of the flood. There were about a dozen pages in it, I think, and I used to sell these to visitors on the buses – just a little memento of that terrible time, really.

Then in 1954 I decided that I'd like to join the AA. I was good with my hands, and knew a bit about engines because I had a couple of motorbikes at the time which I used to work on. Back then there wasn't much to an engine – you had a set of plugs, a set of points, a condenser, a coil, some spark plugs, and if you had petrol it would go! Not much could go wrong! Not like today – cor, you need a computer today to fix a car, don't you?!

To join the AA you had to have an oral test to start with – "What would you do if this happens? What would you do if that happens?" – that sort of thing. When you got through that you were sent off to a big country house in Nottingham and did the training there for a fortnight. There were single rooms there, a gym, a tennis court, a swimming pool – it was a wonderful place. You worked on engines which had faults put on for you to find. There were lectures all day and writing up things at night – often I was still writing things up at midnight!

In those days each AA man had their own patch, which they had to patrol and couldn't leave. My patch was Lynmouth to Porlock via the Toll Road. You drove up and down and, if a member was stopped,

My AA patch was Lynmouth to Porlock.

Snow at the side of the A39 in the winter of '54.

you'd pull up and ask, "Can I help you?" If someone told me that a car had broken down nearby, but off my patch, all I could do was phone one of the garages and they would go out. There were two garages, Central and Pollards, and they were very competitive and I had to make sure I called them first one, then the other. There'd be all hell to pay if I wasn't fair.

There were always plenty of breakdowns. Fan-belts and water hoses were the most common. You couldn't carry spares of all the different fan-belts, so you'd see what was needed and then drive the motorbike down to the garage at Porlock, get it, and then drive back and fit it. The sidecar was there to carry your two gallons of petrol, your foot-pump, the red flags, the first aid box and anything else you needed. Nowadays you can go along that stretch and not see a break-down for weeks, and that's mostly because of the MOT. Back then, if a car started and would go, you were allowed to take it out on the road, and there was all sorts of rubbish out there breaking down left, right and centre! Of course winters were much worse then, far more extreme, and that took a toll on the number of breakdowns, too. I had a motorbike and sidecar for the first ten years I was with the AA, then we had a Mini for about five, then an Austin Gipsy, and after that a yellow Land Rover.

*The water barrels at the AA box for topping up radiators that were
boiling over after coming up Porlock Hill.*

The AA box at Pitcombe Head used to have a series of water
barrels next to it so that cars which were boiling over after coming up
Porlock Hill could top up their radiators. Another of my duties was
to keep those barrels filled up. I'd try to catch as much rain as possible in a line of buckets I had behind the wall there, and if that
wasn't enough I'd have to get a tank of water up to the box and keep
the barrels filled that way. Those barrels were removed long ago but
the box is still there, and there aren't many of those left anywhere in
the country now are there? Shame really.*

Because there was no radio contact in those days, I used to have to
stand at the AA box at Pitcombe Head every day at 11 o'clock and
3 o'clock sharp. This was in case the office needed to contact me.
They would phone me on the phone in the box – it would ring and
I'd pick it up! This was called being "on standby point" and all the
patrolmen had to stand by their boxes at a certain time in the early
days.

Besides patrolling my patch, and being on standby point at the
box, I could stop anywhere or any time I wanted to along the road,
but my AA vehicle had to be visible at all times. I started my day at
nine o'clock each morning and was on duty until lighting-up time,
or seven o'clock, whichever came earlier. There was an hour off for
lunch and we had two ten-minute tea-breaks. I used to try to time my
patrols so that I would be near home at lunch time.

---

* The future of the Pitcombe Head AA box was secured when the Department of the Environ-
ment declared it a listed building.

*We had regular briefings from AA Superintendents
who came round on training visits.*

Another thing we had to do was salute cars as they passed if the driver was a member and they had a badge on the car. I remember I was at the top of Countisbury Hill one time and a car passed with a badge and it was so ingrained in me that I automatically saluted before realising I was off-duty, out of uniform, and pushing a pram!

The RAC and the AA were always in competition, touting for business. If we both saw someone broken down it was whoever got there first – you know, first man there! If the breakdown was a member of the RAC, of course you'd pass them over to him, but if they belonged to neither you'd try to get them to join up with the AA. In fact I signed up 54 new members in my first nine months in the AA, and received a silver AA crested ashtray with

my name engraved on it as an award! Shame – I've given up smoking now, haven't I?!

This one went over at Windwhistle on the A39,
between County Gate and the trees.

Another problem we had to deal with on the roads was the lorries which used to get blown over. That happened quite a lot on my stretch. Back then it wasn't like today, when they close off the road and call out the emergency services; in those days we just used to get on with it ourselves as best we could, with whoever and whatever was there! With the one in the picture above, stakes were put into the ground in the field on the other side of the road, and ropes and winches were used to pull it back on to its wheels again. There was a chap working with a caterpillar tractor near to another one that went over at County Gate and he helped out with that.

The drivers were usually all right – the lorries often went over gently, you see, with the wind sort of cushioning the lorry as it turns over. If the lorry goes over and there is a drop on the other side it isn't so good. I don't mean a big drop – I mean just sloping away a bit. But if it goes over on to a bank the driver will probably hardly notice the jolt! In fact, if they drove faster they probably wouldn't have gone over at all. I suppose they were a bit nervous and went quite slowly and that's how the wind caught them.

This was closer to County Gate itself, which you can see behind the caterpillar tractor.

When the AA phased out the motorbike and sidecar, I was given a Mini. I thought it would be better than being out in all weathers on the bike, but it wasn't! On the bike you were properly dressed; you had your oil-skins on, and a towel round your neck, and you kept dry. When you worked from the Mini, and it was raining, you'd put your mac on and it just wasn't proper protection. It's funny, but you got far more wet working from the Mini.

The biggest change came when they introduced the radio, which was at the same time as the Mini came along, in about 1964. Then you could go anywhere, and patrolmen with individual patches became a thing of the past.

The golden handshake – myself, Barbara and the Big Boy from Bristol, my boss.

I retired after 36 years service and they gave me a big golden hand-shake. They took a photo of the actual handshake, with Barbara in the middle and the Big Boy from Bristol on the right, you know the boss. We stayed the night at the White Hart Hotel, all expenses paid – big meal, and boy did I have a head in the morning!

Council workers on the road above the Blue Ball up at Barna Barrow and …

… looking the other way, to the east, on that same stretch of road.

The snow drifted until it was as high as my house.

I've said before that we used to have terrible winters compared to what we have now. The 1947 winter was one of the worst and I took these photos above the Blue Ball, at the top of Barna Barrow. A chap got stuck and had to walk to the pub and spend the night there. In the morning the Council sent a gang of men to shovel the road and get him out. That's them all digging him out there. He wasn't an important man, just a Joe Bloggs who got snowed in, and the Council had to get him out. That's their job – to keep the roads clear.

Then in 1962/63 we had the famous winter that everyone still talks about. The snow continued to drift until it was as high as my house! After a couple of days it packed down hard and you could walk over it without sinking in. The animals, if they weren't buried, would just walk over the gates, or over the hedges on top of the snow, and from one field to the next.

The Lynmouth to Porlock road was blocked for eight weeks and three days – nothing went through for all that time. Then they managed to get it cleared from Lynmouth to the top here at Countisbury, and the lorries could get in from Barnstaple as far as here, but no further. So this became the pick-up point for the helicopters that dropped supplies and animal feed to all the outlying places beyond here. The lorries would pull in next to the field just beyond the

church and throw the bags over the hedge, and they'd load them on to the helicopter and start the air-lift from there.

The picture above is of the Trilly Gate, immediately opposite to where the air-lift was carried out. You can see what conditions were like. Nowadays I'm sometimes reminded of how deep the snow was when I drive past my old AA box at Pitcombe Head. I'm told that it was completely buried. Have a look next time you pass and imagine it all.

Interviewed July 2008

Roy Kellaway

Roy spent the first forty years of his life at River View, Brendon; he was born there in 1926, grew up and spent the first part of his married life there. His father was the village baker, and his mother ran the grocery shop. From an early age he was involved with horses, first in his father's stables, then at the Staghunters' stables, and then as groom and second horse to the Master of Staghounds. In 1951 he married Dee – Doreen Wells – daughter of a dental surgeon from Bristol, who had been evacuated with her family to Oare Manor. They have two sons, Norman and Gordon, who both farm, and four grand-children.

MY GRANDPARENTS on my mother's side were Dan Gregory and his wife Lucy. He was known by everybody as Farmer Dan; all the farmers in those days were called "Farmer Such-and-such" as a sort of mark of respect. Originally they farmed the Lorna Doone Farm and that is where mother had been born. Then they moved nearer to Brendon and took on Coombe Farm. Farmer Dan died when I was five or six, so I never really knew him. His was one of the last funerals in Brendon where he was buried from his own house, and it took eight sets of six men to carry the coffin all the way up to the church. That's 48 men, working in relays.

His speciality was making hayricks, which was a very skilful job. You had to look at the amount of hay while it was still in the field and judge from that just how big the base of the stack needed to be; it was no good running out of hay or having too much, you had to have just the right amount to finish the rick. Then you built the stack with its walls sloping outwards slightly, to shed the water. If the hay wasn't completely dry you'd have to build a chimney in the middle, because it would heat up like a compost heap and that heat had to get out. They'd have a sack of grass in the middle on a rope, which they'd pull up slowly as they built it up, and that left the hole for the chimney. It was finished with a sloping roof which was thatched with rushes from the common, or with wheat-straw. Done properly, the hay would easily last a couple of years in a good rick.

There's an early photograph taken by Mr Vowles of haymaking in Big Lee, the field in Brendon on the left before you get to the Staghunters. It was turned into a postcard and had the title "'Tis lovely hay down Brendon way." Well, Farmer Dan is the one on top of the half-made rick in that photograph and my sister Olive is sitting in the foreground: she's the third girl along from the left. It was taken before I was born, and roughly where the bungalow is now.

We used to have another lovely photograph of all the Brendon farmers at the bottom of Porlock Hill with their horses and carts, but we lost that in the flood. The farmers used to have to get extra straw from Porlock because they couldn't grow enough up here. They'd all go down together, and use each other's horses to double up and get the carts back up Porlock Hill. They all went down together and made a day of it!

The "'Tis lovely hay down Brendon way" postcard taken by Vowles.
Grandfather Dan is on the half-made rick, and sister Olive
third from the left in the foreground.

Grandfather Dan on a tedder in the same field
before they started making the ricks.

Dad originally came to Brendon in about 1908. He came up from
Holsworthy to Brendon as the gardener and groom to a family called
Hood who lived at Brendon House. The garden there was at the front,
where the car park is now, and all round the side too, and it was an
absolutely fabulous garden. Well, he soon met my mother and they

were married and had four daughters – Dorothy, Freda, Olive and Edna. I think they were desperate for a boy because I was born last of all, and much later. On the day I was born Dad was out delivering bread in his pony and cart, and Farmer Dan knew that the bread round went past the Blue Ball up at Countisbury. So he walked from Brendon up to the Blue Ball with the news that Father had his longed-for son at last! Grandfather was probably about seventy when he rushed up there that day! I don't think they got home too early that night! My sisters were all a lot older than I was; to give you an idea, the oldest one, Dot was about eighteen years older than me. In fact she was married and had her first child the day before I was born, so I've got a niece who's one day older than me!

During the Great War Dad was in the Army and was in Palestine. He was also in India, it seems, because the only picture I have of him is in his uniform, and the name of the photographer is at the bottom of the photo: "M Doss and Bros, Madras". He came back from the war with malaria, which he suffered from for the rest of his life. The family were living at Rose Cottage in Brendon before the war, and after it too.

Then in 1924 Sir Edward Mountain sold the Brendon Estates, and River View, where the Brendon Bakery and stables were, came up for sale along with the field at the back. It was at that point that Dad bought the place and took over the bakery; he took it over from the Barrows. My parents also opened a shop in the same building, a grocery shop, and Mother would run the shop side of things while Dad was the baker. As you looked at the building, the stables were on the left, where we kept the horses and the cart for delivering the bread. Then behind the stables, and on the side of the house, was the bakery. The shop was in the front of the building, in the middle, and stuck out towards the road. Our house was on the right-hand end of the building, and we'd have to go in through the shop to get into the house.

There was no sign outside the grocery shop, and there wasn't any room on the street in front to put things, but everyone knew it was the shop. We sold all the everyday groceries that people needed – as well as cigarettes and sweets, of course. Over time Mother got to know her customers pretty well and she knew what they usually had; in fact, she'd sometimes remind them if they forgot something they usually asked for, especially if they'd walked miles to get there!

As you came into the shop there was a big wooden counter on the right-hand side, and all the goods were on shelves behind that and on two tables along the front wall. All the loose stuff stood on the floor in sacks and Mother was for-ever weighing things out. The cash went into a little pull-out cash drawer. The shop opened any time after about seven o'clock in the morning; somebody would rap on the door and you'd open the shop, and it would shut at about six o'clock in the evening, but it could always re-open if anybody wanted something later that night! There was a bell on the door of the shop and that meant Mother and my sisters could get on helping in the bakery, or with the visitors' rooms, if no one was in the shop.

*Mother towards the
end of her life.*

99

There was also another shop in Brendon at that time, which was run by the Barrows. They sold cigarettes and sweets, that sort of thing. They sold newspapers too, but not the *Western Morning News* or the *Devon and Exeter Gazette,* which were only sold by us. We had an agreement with the Barrows that they wouldn't sell those two papers. Each shop had their own customers, who'd go regularly to the same shop. They probably had more kids going to them than we did because they sold a cheaper range of sweets than Mother had, and kids like to get as much as they can for their money, don't they?!

We didn't do any deliveries from the shop and customers would come into Brendon from quite a wide area. For example, people would come in from all the outlying areas on a pony with a list and stock up. Mother kept no record of what she had in the shop. No accounts were kept or anything like that. She just had it all in her head.

When he retired, Grandfer Dan became shepherd to Mr Pile.
That's him and me in the field beyond Millslade the year before he died.

We also had three rooms upstairs where Mother would take in visitors. I'm not sure when she first started but I expect it was about the same time as they bought the place, in 1924 – to help pay for it, probably! An advertisement appears in the *Homelands Guide to Lynton and Lynmouth* which came out in about 1925 or 1926, so she had started it by then. We've still got one of the Visitors' Books and it starts in 1931. The first entry is from a London lady who says, "Going back to town after a short week-end, about my 70th time of staying with Mrs Kellaway," so you can see she had certainly been doing it quite some time by 1931!

In the bakery, the biggest thing, of course, was the oven, a steam oven, which took up the whole back room. It was about fifteen foot square and stood off the floor on short pillars. The lower part of it was the proving oven and the main oven was above that. It was made of iron and was all

---

BOARD RESIDENCE OR BED AND BREAKFAST

Moderate Terms.

Also Hunters, Hacks and Children's Ponies for Hire.

"River View," Brendon
On River Lyn.

Mrs. Kellaway, "River View."

---

bolted together; I know that because in later years, when Father gave up the baking, he sold it to Gillbank and Squires the grocer/baker at Lynton. They came down and unbolted it and took it away in pieces.

There was another room next to the oven with a giant wooden table and this is where all the bakery work was done. This is where the bread tins were (Dad only baked bread, nothing else) and the wooden trough where all the dough was mixed. That trough was about six feet long by three feet wide!

Dad's routine was always the same. Five o'clock in the morning he'd wake up. He had no alarm clock, he'd just wake at five. He'd get up, light the fire in the oven and then he'd have his cup of tea. Then he mixed the dough in the wooden trough. The flour was Rank's Flour and it was delivered to the bakery in sacks; three or four of these sacks would go in. The water came from the well, which was over the road – there was no sink in the bakery. It was a dip well and we shared it with all the neighbours. Then he mixed this dough by hand, which was very heavy work. The tins were greased with lard, which Father used to get from Mother next door in the shop.

Then my sisters and mother would join him and help. They'd get the dough on to the table, cut it into sections, roll it out and knead it, and then weigh it on the scales. I remember there was always a penny and a ha'penny on one side of the scales as well as the weights, and this extra weight was to allow for the evaporation of the bread as it cooked. Otherwise Father would be selling underweight loaves. That old penny and ha'penny stayed on those scales for years and years, they were always there! Then they'd put the dough into the tins and the tins into the oven, with a long wooden shovel called a "peel" which could reach right to the back. Then it was breakfast time!

Olive and Mother pitching up a load of hay to Father. We had the field called Abbey Close at the back of River View.

Olive would have harnessed up the horse and cart so it was ready to start the delivery round after breakfast. It was about eleven o'clock by the time the bread was cooked and they'd loaded up the cart. He used to have two rounds, the Lynton round and the Oare round, and he'd alternate them each day. The Lynton route was Rockford, Brendon Barton, Barbrook, Lynton, Lynmouth and Countisbury, delivering all along the way. The Oare route was Southernwood, Oare and Oare Manor, Oareford, then over Robber's Bridge and up the common to Lilycombe, Broomstreet, Yearnor, Yenworthy, County Gate, Ashton, Wellfield; the Glenthorne bread was left in a box at the top of the lane, and then home. Both routes used to take him until about nine or ten o'clock at night before he got back. He'd do the baking and the deliveries five days a week. Wednesday was a day at home when he could work in the garden, which was about a quarter of an acre. Sunday was a day of rest!

Meanwhile Olive would set off on the pony-round to the farms with a sack of loaves across the saddle, bulging out on both sides, and she had two routes too, which she'd alternate, same as Father. One was up to Crossgate, then Tippacott, Shilstone, Cranscombe and home. The other route was Coombe, Wilsham, Dewcombe, Desolate and back.

Father'd probably make about seventy loaves a day, almost all of them white – people used to like white bread in those days – but he'd also do some brown loaves too because the hotels liked to be able to offer people a choice and would take some brown. The only competition, really, was Gillbanks and Squires at Lynton, but Dad delivered this side of Lynton and they delivered the opposite way.

Olive setting off to deliver bread to the farms with a sack of loaves across the saddle.

As a child I was allowed the little corners of dough at the end of the weighing, the off-cuts, and I used to make gingerbread men which turned out brown when they were cooked. On occasion Dad would cook a large joint for the British Legion dinner and other big-scale things like that.

Then one night the shafts on the cart broke when Dad was on the Oare round. He had just left Ashton when it happened. The horse bolted and he hung on to the reins and was wrenched out of the cart. Well, fortunately the horse headed for home, and the blacksmith, Charley Squires, and Fred Groves at Leeford saw it coming down Combe Girt Hill and realised something had happened. They went up the hill on their motorbikes to the road at the top, where they came across Bert Ash walking along with two cart shafts over his shoulders. The three of them then found Dad, who had managed to get to Wellfield, and they all got him and his undelivered loaves home.

He gave up the bakery soon after that. The thing that made him finally decide to give up was the increased motor cars on the road, and especially the charabancs.* Church Road, which led up to Brendon Church, was very narrow and there were no passing places. The charabancs used to come down the hill on a regular basis and it was too steep for them to reverse up, so every time Dad met one he was the one who'd have to back the horse and cart down the hill. That's a very difficult thing, to get a horse to go backwards and to keep the cart going straight. Well, after this started happening most days he'd had enough; that was the final straw, if you like, and he

Mother opposite River View, at the wall.
The communal well was just behind her there, below the wall.
It's got wooden railings now and the well has been filled in.

* The very early open-topped buses.

104

Mother and Father on the left, and me holding the horse. In the cart is the Rev Marshall with his two grandsons. On the right is Ede Floyd from Oaklands, who was nursemaid to the two boys. The Rev Marshall was Vicar of Oare and Culbone and was taking his two grandsons on a sightseeing tour. He came to us to hire the horse and cart.

decided to give up baking. He sold the oven to Gillbank and Squires, who started selling bread in this area, and then later Wonderloaf took over and delivered their bread everywhere in vans. And that was the end of the small-scale bakers.

So in about 1935, instead of the bakery, Dad started up a riding stable and soon we had a sign up outside River View: "Kellaway's Riding Stables". We already had some stables there from the bakery, and he rented the stables from the Staghunters, too, so when it reached its peak I suppose we had about twenty-four horses and ponies in total. Olive was good with the horses and she started helping there, and Freda stayed home helping Mother indoors with the shop and the visitors. Some of our own visitors used to hire horses from us, and of course all the people at the Staghunters would use our stables too. In those days people used to come down for riding holidays and they'd spend all their time riding, not like now when most people just go for an odd ride during the time they're here. In those days, too, there were many more people who could ride properly; people who were true horsemen, if you like. Often now you get people who've never been out on a horse before, they just want to try riding.

The communal well at Brendon was opposite River View and right next to the river, but it was a spring-fed well: the water came from a spring and not the river. It was used by everybody at our end of the village: the mill, the shop, Weir Cottage, the two villas, River View and River View Cottage. It was a dip-well – you'd dip your bucket into it and fill it up that way. There was always a dispute about the little bit of land the well was on and who owned it, or whether it was common land. Disputes and court cases about this rumbled on for years.

Harry Richards with two jugs of water which he'd just dipped in the well. That's me sitting on the bank there with my two nieces, Daphne and Joan Barrow. Harry was an older brother of Stanley Richards who owned Brendon Mill.

River View used to have its own well behind the bakery, an eighteen foot well, and every time the springs broke that well would flood and flow into the river. Well, Dad had a brainwave and decided to turn our well into a private sanitation system. He had the toilet and waste pipes all flow into our well, and then each time the springs broke it drained into the river! In those days all the waste went into the river anyway, but ours went in automatically! We had one of the first flush toilets for miles around, I imagine!

I can remember him having the toilets converted because he had an old fellow dig the trench across the back garden for the pipes. Dad had two beautiful rose bushes, one yellow and the other white, and each was about ten feet across. Well, the fellow cut them both down for his trench and Dad went absolutely bananas! "I thought they was just a couple of old thorns!" he said to Dad!

Roy in his best outfit with pet dog Spud in about 1938.

We were lucky in Brendon to have electricity up at our end of the village quite early on. It came from a water turbine in the mill-stream that came from Leeford to the Brendon Mill. All the houses from Brendon Mill down to Millslade were connected to this supply and it used to be turned on in the evenings; the sluice was at Leeford Bridge and would be opened and the water would flow through the turbine. Then the sluice was closed at some point, and that was your electricity for the night! How bright your lights were depended on how many other people had their lights on at the same time! Sometimes you needed a candle just to see if your electrics were actually on! It was Grandfather whose job it was to open and close those sluices. Later they fitted a generator at Millslade, which was more efficient, and they used all the same wiring to the houses but just sent the current the other way!

The Brendon Mill was a saw-mill and they also did a little corn-grinding on a stone, which they could work as well as the saws. The timber used to come in from the Glenthorne estate by horse and cart, and be piled up to the right of the buildings. On the other side of the river was a big shed with open slats and that's where all the timber was left to dry, or "cure", as they used to say. It used to make quite a racket when the saw started up, and I remember one time Edna was on her horse and the sawing started and spooked the horse, which threw her. The Brendon Mill was known as Richard's Mill and Stanley Richards, the owner, lived at the Old Rectory* when he was first married.

During my schooldays I used to help with the horses. I had to go up and catch the ponies each morning from the fields, and if there was one you couldn't catch it made you late for school. Miss Beck was not thrilled by this. I'd also sometimes go out on rides if they were very busy, to show people where to go on the common. Often, too, in the evenings in the summer, I'd be detailed to go to the harness room to clean stirrup irons or something before I was able to go down to the recreation ground – where the village hall and car park is now – and play with the other kids.

Talking of the recreation ground reminds me of playing cricket there. At that time the BBC's "Children's Hour" on the wireless was hosted by a man called Mr Brian Mickey. Well, who do you think came down to Brendon one summer but Mr Brian Mickey himself! I think he stayed at Millslade and I remember all of us kids playing cricket in the evenings with him there on the recreation ground. He was a great big fellow with a big character, too – about fifty years of age, I should imagine! Another person who came down – I think this was during the war – was the famous band leader Victor Sylvester. He came down one summer and took Peace Cottage, beyond Countisbury Mill. Another strong memory of summer was the cream teas that all the village kids were invited to at the Palmers' farm at Leeford when they were doing the shearing there – a very posh show that was, all laid on just for us village kids!

At about this time one year there were an awful lot of caterpillars on the redcurrants and Dad detailed Edna and myself to go out and pick them all off. Well, we had a cardboard box about a foot square,

---

* The Old Rectory is now called Deercombe. The Rev Day was the incumbent before the Rev Jenkins, who used to live at Combe Park.

*Prize-giving at the Brendon Show – me collecting one of my riding prizes!
On the left is David Pile from Hallslake, then the Rev Rex Jenkins from
Combe Park. Miss Halliday from Glenthorne has her back to the
camera and next to her is Walter Lang, who farmed Farley.*

Spud showing off on my show-pony Misty.

which we slowly filled full of caterpillars, and then we went back to Dad to show what we'd done. Somehow we got into an argument about who'd picked off the most and I was losing. In my frustration I hit the bottom of the box; I whacked it and all the caterpillars flew out all over Edna. I've never got out of an argument quicker in my life! My father had a very short fuse and I shot off, I can tell you! I never went back for at least a couple of hours! That was my first experience of gardening!

We used to have gardening as one of the lessons at school – I remember the lesson was just called "Gard'nin"! As country kids we'd all learnt a bit from our parents, and when we went to school we each had a little plot of land given to us to cultivate and timetabled lessons to do it in. There was a prize for the best patch, and the head gardener from Glenthorne and Donald Graham from Wilsham would came up to the school in July to judge whose patch was best. The prize was a pocketknife. I remember I grew everything there, everything except kidney beans, and I just missed out on that first prize!

Many of us were quite young when we first tried smoking; actually we didn't smoke cigarettes at all when we first started. Cow parsley, which we used to call "billards", has a big old stem that's hollow and those stems dried out like sticks. Well that's what we used to smoke, the girls as well as the boys. We'd light up one of these old billard stalks – and stink like anything, they did, and blow your head off as well! Then I progressed on to the Woodbines. They came in packs of five and would disappear on occasion from the shop – not too often, of course, or you'd be caught. I didn't smoke regularly, though, until I was about sixteen.

One of my favourite things at school was the singing, and each year we'd have a concert in the room at the back of the Staghunters. These concerts were very, very well attended – everyone in the area would be there. The teachers would play the piano and we'd sing and act. Well, in the last year at school, during a public performance, I was singing "Somewhere Over the Rainbow", which goes to a very high note, and as I hit the note my voice cracked – I croaked out that high note in front of all those people! I've always said that that's when my voice broke – somewhere over the rainbow at the Staghunters!

One of my least favourite things was Sundays. As a kid you'd have to go to Sunday School in the morning up at Countisbury, which was run by our normal teacher, Miss Beck. Then after lunch you'd go to the other Sunday School at the reading room* below Deercombe, and that was run by the Rev Jenkins. Then at six o'clock there was the Brendon Church service, which you'd go to too. I think we kids were sent up there to keep us out of the way, because not a lot of local people went, even in those days. Brendon was a farming area so a lot of the farmers couldn't get to go. It wasn't like years ago when the Squire said you had to go to church. Very few went to church and I remember the Rev Jenkins stopping the service occasionally to tell us to stop rustling our sweet papers.

Another thing I didn't enjoy very much was when we got the cane at school! Mrs Beck used to whack us across the hand, not on the palm but across the open fingers, which was worse! I remember one time some of the kids had got up to something down at Brendon, and

*My brother-in-law and his brother riding through Brendon.
They were extras in the film* Lorna Doone!

* All that remains of the old reading room below Deercombe are the roofless gable ends, still clearly visible from the road. It had been a lively centre for local people – an alternative to the Staghunters and the Rockford – open most evenings, with a kitchen and a fire that was lit every evening by Frank Lethaby. It had a three-quarter size snooker table and, among other activities, whist drives were held there on a regular basis. Everyone who lived to the north of the reading room would return home in the dark up what was the old road to the left of Deercombe – now a public path – to the top lane near Tippacott, where they would then go their separate ways. Likewise, those at Wilsham would take the path up through the woods, opposite the Rockford pub.

The Dunster show, 1939.
That year the show was on the same day that Hitler invaded Poland,
Friday 1st September. Three days later, on Sunday the third,
Britain had declared war. I won best horse in my class!

when we arrived at school next morning Mrs Beck already knew about it. She kept all the Brendon children over a certain age out in the playground and asked the guilty ones to own up. When that didn't produce results, she just caned us all – both boys and girls – one by one as we filed into the classroom! I must have been about seven or eight when that happened!

Clearing the ground at Countisbury School, ready to dig the air-raid shelter. That's me third from the right with the shiny boots and leggings on. First on the left is John Hoyles, and the one next to him is an evacuee kid.

When the war started I was in my last year at Countisbury, and one of the first things we did was to dig out an air-raid shelter in the school grounds. That area in the picture above was dug into a huge hole deep enough for all the kids to fit into – about twenty-five of us, and both the teachers! We built stone walls inside the shelter and covered everything with big poles and galvanised iron, and the roof with earth. Miss Beck cancelled afternoon lessons each day and I remember we went out and dug until it was done. We heard the German bombers flying over and heard them bombing Cardiff, so we all knew what the dangers were. We had air-raid practice drill: you filed out of the classroom in an orderly fashion, you did not rush … you know the style, but we never had to use the shelter for real. There were no lights, no candles or anything inside, and no furniture or supplies, just a bare earth floor.

113

I also remember all the road signs being removed so that the Germans wouldn't know where they were if they landed. That meant a lot of people suddenly started getting lost – a lot of the visitors used to get lost and had to ask the way; they didn't know where they were going, unless of course they knew the area!

Another thing we used to do at this time was go to the Methodist Chapel below Deercombe, where they gave magic lantern shows. You'd pay something at the door and go and see the slide show. It was always a religious topic but it was something different to do, and wonderful for us kids to see a great screen like that with pictures on. There were only about four Methodists in Brendon; I think all the rest of the congregation must have come in from the outlying areas. In fact it was outside that chapel that I heard that war had been declared. I was going up Chapel Steep – the little hill next to the chapel – and I met Jim Moore and he was the one who told me.*

The war meant a lot more work for Mother and Freda in the shop, because they had to collect all the ration book coupons from everybody and send them off with each order. As the war went on and

Roy cutting grass in a field at Fellingscott.

* On the same day Dee, Roy's future wife (who he hadn't yet met) was at the Sacred Heart Church on the outskirts of Bristol when "The Rev. Father interrupted the service at eleven o'clock and said that war had been declared and that everybody should go home. This we did."

things got harder, I know Mother would always try and share things out between all the customers. If there was extra she'd try to give three times as much to a family of three, for example, than she gave to a family of one. I remember her talking about this quite often.

I only came across one conscientious objector and he was living with the Crocombe family at Lee Cottage. They were Methodists and had him in lodging with them. I don't know what his name was but I bought a pair of patent leather dancing shoes from him! I've no idea why he had them in the first place because he didn't agree with dancing, but I paid him a pound, and very nice they were too!

Towards the end of Dad's baking days, my sister Edna and I would deliver the bread on the pony if for some reason Olive couldn't do it. That's the main reason we used to go up and visit the outlying farms. The other reason for visiting those places was to hand-deliver telegrams, which us lads would be paid to do by the postman. We'd get 6d for the outlying places: Cranscombe was 6d and Broomstreet was 6d, for example; and for the closer places we'd get 3d. It was quite common for telegrams to be very local; we often delivered telegrams from Lynton saying that someone had got the train up from Barnstaple (the miniature railway) and could they be collected from the station. This was before telephones were common, you know: us lads would be rushing about the countryside with all these hand-delivered messages!

The first proper job I had on leaving school was with a Welsh timber firm called Edwards, hauling logs out of Barton Wood with a horse and chains. We had three heavy-breed carthorses: two came over from Wales and Father bought one himself, a shire-horse. That's all we did with it – haul logs out of those steep woods. Those big horses used to be on all the farms but were becoming redundant at this time, with the tractors coming in. You'd often see them in fields, retired if you like; people would let them live out their lives in odd fields.

We'd stack the logs by the road on Ash Plain, which is the flat part at the bottom of Church Hill, and a lorry would then take them from there to the railway at Minehead. From Minehead all the poor stuff went over to Wales for pit props and the good stuff was kept for furniture. At the end of each week we'd load the lorry on the Friday, and then on the following evening as many as wanted would travel from Brendon to Minehead, clinging to the logs on the back of the lorry. We'd unload them into a railway truck, then we'd get out of our

Dee aged ten with her mum.

overalls, have a scrub-up and all go to the Regal Ballroom for the night! Afterwards we'd return to Brendon the same way – on the back of the lorry. If there were any girls with us, they'd travel in luxury in the cab!

Meanwhile my future wife Dee – Doreen was her proper name, Doreen Wells – and her family had arrived as evacuees from Bristol and were all staying at Oare Manor with Mr Nancekivell. She was ten when she arrived. Her father was a dentist in Bristol and they had all been down here on holiday just before the war, in the summer of 1939. Well, in 1940, when the bombing started in Bristol in earnest, they all came back to Oare Manor as evacuees – although we have never really thought of them as that. They were at Oare Manor for one Christmas, with her dad travelling backwards and forwards from here to Bristol. She used to call Mr Nancekivell "Uncle Bob" and his wife "Mrs N". She doesn't remember much about the Manor except one time when Mr Nancekivell led a pony in through the front door, up the stairs, across the landing, and then down the stairs the other side and out. He used to do things like that after he'd had the odd drink! That shows his character, really; he was a strong character who would do things on the spur of the moment – often without thinking about the consequences! They had farm staff and stable staff but in the house Mrs N was the cook and she did all that herself. When they went up to Cloud she ran the tea gardens up there and took in visitors – she was very much a hands-on sort of lady.

Then Dee's dad bought Oaremead, the farm opposite Oare Manor, and the family went to live there and her Dad started doing a bit of farming as a sideline. Dee went to a convent at Minehead as a weekly boarder; two of her sisters went to other schools as full-time boarders.

After buying Oaremead, Dee's father rented Fellingscott and Tippacott, and he put my sister Olive and her husband Tom Rawle into Fellingscott as managers. It was they who offered me work

Dee at Oarmead.

there. That's how I started farming, by working at Fellingscott and Tippacott.

And it was at Fellingscott that I met Dee. It was harvest time and she came over to generally help out. She had a twin sister called Eileen, who was identical; and, the snag was, back in those days I could never be sure which one I was with! Anyway, it developed from there, much to her Dad's disgust. Back in those days a dental surgeon didn't expect his eldest daughter

117

to date a farm labourer, I suppose. He wasn't very pleased, to put it mildly! Well, at the same time we were planning to get married, Dee's twin sister planned to get married as well. We thought we'd have a double wedding and all got married at Minehead when Doreen and Eileen both turned twenty-one.

We started married life down at Brendon, in the cottage next to River View, but Mother was lonely; she'd always had people living with her, and we soon moved back in with her. She was with us for the rest of her life. Mother was the most sensible person you could ever really wish to meet. She was a strong character and always seemed to be busy. She never let things worry her. She said that, if something was going to happen, it would happen, and that was that, worrying wouldn't help – and that really rubbed off on me. I've never been the worrying type!

Then, of course, came the 1952 flood. Each time the river was in flood you'd always have a certain amount of trees coming down. When this happened it was a custom in Brendon for everybody to go down to Millslade Bridge, the footbridge, and watch there, because that was always the first bridge to go. A tree would come down, branches first, get caught on the bridge; the trunk would get swept on and the bridge would rise up in the air and then crumple. It always

Millslade Bridge, always the first to go when the river was in flood.
The sign said "Do not feed the fish" but everybody did!

Clearing up outside River View after the flood.

happened the same way and it was a sort of tradition for everyone to go to Millslade Bridge when the water suddenly rose in the river.

Well, on the evening of the flood in 1952 we had fed our visitors, and we knew the water was rising fast so we all went down to watch the bridge go, which it very soon did. We turned round to come home just as it was getting dark. By this time the water was over the road and something hit me on the leg. I reached down and we realised it was our own folding screen – a six-foot-high folding screen which had been washed out of our house! Well, we got back pretty quick, I can tell you, and lifted the settee on top of the table to try to save it, but it was all a bit pointless. The water kept rising and in the end reached up to the ninth stair on the staircase. We spent the night there, just sitting at the top of the stairs, watching.

The next morning the water went back down as quickly as it came up. Out in the street it was devastation: there was stuff everywhere. Ernie Barrow's car had been washed away; it had just floated off downstream somewhere and was a write-off. The bottom of Lee Villas opposite to us had been washed out a bit and Mother and I moved a cart that had wedged itself in the doorway there and went into the house. We shouted and there was no reply, so we went up the stairs and Billy Crocombe, who was Mother's cousin, and about eighty years old, was in bed fast asleep with his white beard tucked

The two boys and me on the Fergie TE20 in front of Lee Villas, and our son Norman shifting lambs on the farm.

out just over the sheets and his hat still on! He'd slept through it all and didn't know his downstairs had flooded to about six feet as he lay asleep! It took weeks to clean up and for everything to dry out.

After we married I gradually took on a bit of land and started farming. The boys, Norman and Gordon, were born. Over the next ten years or so I built up the farming side of things. The owner of the land assured me that when the time came I could buy it off them and I put a lot of my own re-sources into it. Then the owner's husband died and the land was put up with the house and both offered for sale together. I was the coffin-bearer one day and received my eviction the next. We couldn't afford both the house and the land, so that was that: good-bye to my income as a farmer. I had to find something else to do and that's when I took on the Staghunters' stables. I was the groom at the Staghunters and ran that for a couple of years.

*During the time I was groom at the Staghunters
I had to look neat and tidy at all times!*

Then I became groom and second-horseman up at Cloud Farm
to Bob Nancekivell, who was Master of the Staghounds. We'd go out
hunting two or three days each week. On the other days I looked after
the horses, getting them shod and so on. I wore a uniform every day
which was supplied for me, a jacket and breeches, all black with a
little bit of a white fleck in it. On hunt days I'd get his horses ready
and transport them to wherever the meet was, and then have everything waiting and ready for him for when he arrived, which was usually by car. The nearest meets were at the Staghunters or at County
Gate; the furtherest probably at Raleigh's Cross up in the Brendons.
On a typical day I'd go up to Cloud on my motorbike and then take
the horses by lorry to arrive and be ready for an eleven o'clock start

for stag-hunting, or a 10.45 start for hind-hunting. The hunt staff at Exford would in the meantime bring the hounds up, and waited with them in the lorry or in a barn. Then the Harbourer took the tufters out; when he returned to get the pack we were off!

Mr Nancekivell, Master of Hounds, on the left, and me riding second-horse at the back.

It was my job then to ride alongside Mr Nancekivell on the second horse and always have it available. He was a big, heavy chap and he'd ride his horse hard while I took it easy on my horse, taking short-cuts whenever possible to where I thought the stag was going. Then we'd change horses to give the first one a rest. Perhaps we'd change two or three times during the course of a day. I got to know Exmoor extremely well, of course. The secret was to watch the local farmer, who knew his own land; there was always a local man who knew all the short-cuts, and the secret was knowing who that man was and watching him. Years of riding the common, too, on outings from Father's stables, had built up my knowledge of the moor, which helped. The trouble was, I'd sometimes get the short-cut wrong and they all went the other way, and then miles separated me from the Boss. Then I'd had it! Mr Nancekivell had a quick temper, a very quick temper, but I have to say he was always a fair man. If we had a falling-out he'd call me all the names under the sun – he'd say what he wanted to and get it out of his system; and then, an hour later, it was as if nothing had happened. I couldn't tell you the number of times I was given the sack during the day, but by the evening it was all completely forgotten!

I was with him between 1962 and 1966 and I always called him "Boss". I seldom spoke because it didn't pay to speak much: "A know-naught fool is better than a know-all fool" is the Exmoor saying, and it's very true! You didn't offer an opinion unless you were absolutely dead certain you were right. The other hunt staff from Exford were great, they were brilliant; it was a job where we spent a lot of time hanging about, waiting, and we all used to play cards a lot. I thoroughly enjoyed those years and was sorry when I finally left.

Years before, a chap called Geoff Ward had said that, if he bought a place, would I work for him? and I'd agreed. I'd been with Bob Nancekivell for four years when Geoff got a place over at Loxhore. Would I join him? Well, I kept my word and gave in my notice, and that was the end of our Brendon days. It was in 1966 that we moved out of Brendon for good.

Interviewed May 2009

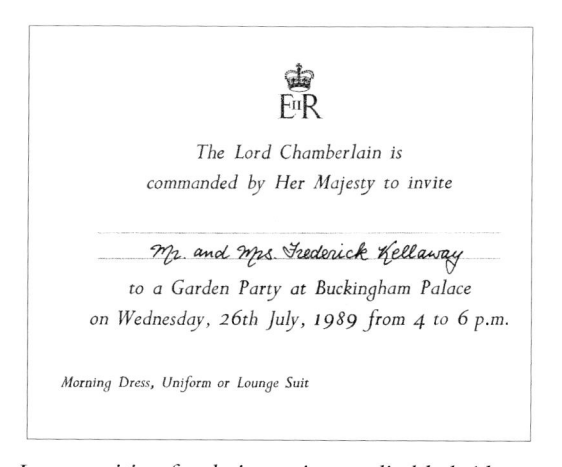

*In recognition for their services to disabled riders,
Roy and Dee were invited to a Garden Party at
Buckingham Palace in 1989.*

123

Bibliography

Roger Burton, *The Heritage of Exmoor*, privately published, 1989.

C.S. Orwin, *The Reclamation of Exmoor Forest*, 1929.

John Frederick Chanter, *A History of the Parishes of Lynton and Countisbury*, 1907.

J.L.W. Page, *An Exploration of Exmoor*, 1890.

Dr Thomas Henry Cooper, *Cooper's Guide to Lynton, Lynmouth…*, 1853.

The Exmoor Oral History Archive at www.somerset.gov.uk/archives/exmoor

Other writers well worth tracking down, in addition to those cited below, are F.J. Snell, A.G. Bradley, Sheracombe, S.H. Burton and Hope Bourne.

References

Page

11 Hazel Riley and Robert Wilson-North, *The Field Archaeology of Exmoor*, English Heritage, 2001.

C.S. Orwin, *The Reclamation of Exmoor Forest*, Oxford University Press, 1929.

16 John Travis, *An Illustrated History of Lynton and Lynmouth*, Breedon Books, 1995.

Charles G. Harper, *The North Devon Coast*, Chapman and Hall, 1908.

35 John Travis, as above.

44 In conversation with Ted Lethaby, June 2009, and shopkeepers in Butcher's Row.

48 In conversation with John Pile, June 2009.

54 In conversation with Ivy Archer, September 2007.

56 Dorothy Hartley, *The Land of England*, Macdonald and Jane, 1979.

65 In conversation with Ted Lethaby, June 2009, and Ben Halliday.

W.H. Thornton, *Reminiscences and Reflections of an Old West-country Clergyman*, 1897.

67 In conversation with Ted Lethaby, June 2009.

68 Cicely Elaine Cooper, *Memoirs of Selworthy*, The Wessex Press, 1951.

75 In conversation with Ted Lethaby, September 2010.

111 In conversation with Ted Lethaby, June 2009, and Gerald Down, January 2008.

Index